Zambia

An assessment of Zambia's structural adjustment experience

Roger Young
and
John Loxley

Revised Edition

The North-South Institute

The Institute is a non-profit corporation established in 1976 to provide professional, policy-relevant research on the 'North-South' issues of relations between industrialized and developing countries. The results of this research are made available to policy makers, interested groups and the general public to help generate greater understanding and informed discussion of development questions. The Institute is independent and non-partisan, and cooperates with a wide range of Canadian, overseas and international organizations working in related activities.

The contents of this paper represent the views and findings of the authors alone and not necessarily those of the North-South Institute's directors or supporters, or those consulted in its preparation.

Canadian Cataloguing in Publication Data

Young, Roger, 1949-
  Zambia: an assessment of Zambia's structural adjustment experience
Rev. ed.
Includes bibliographical references.
ISBN 0-921942-10-9

1. Zambia — Economic policy. Zambia —
Economic conditions — I. Loxley, John, 1942 —
II. North-South Institute (Ottawa, Ont.)
III. Title.

HC915.Y69 1990   338.96894   C90-090469-0

Editor: Edith Carter
Production: Edith Carter
Desktop publishing: Anne Chevalier, Marise Galvani

© The North-South Institute/L'Institut Nord-Sud, 1990

Price: $12.00 (NS-156)

Additional copies may be ordered from the Institute at
55 Murray Street, Suite 200
Ottawa, Canada
K1N 5M3
Telephone: (613) 236-3535   Fax: (613) 237-7435

Contents

Acknowledgements

The North-South Institute wishes to acknowledge the invaluable assistance extended to John Loxley by John Kofi Baffoe of the University of Manitoba in conducting the field work for this study in Zambia in November/December, 1988. The help of Bob Pim of the Canadian High Commission, Lusaka, of Kaj Persson of the Swedish Embassy, Lusaka, and of Roger Young and Marcia Burdette in Ottawa is also acknowledged, without implicating them in any way. Thanks are also due to a large number of Zambian officials and aid agency personnel in Zambia who took time off from pressing duties to assist in data collection and explication, and especially John Sinclair of the Anglophone Africa Division of CIDA, for sponsoring the project.

The Institute gratefully acknowledges the financial contribution of the Canadian International Development Agency to the project on Structural Adjustment.

Preface

In the range of experience with structural adjustment, Zambia has been a controversial country for several years. The challenge of trying to alter its economy, so dependent on copper and other minerals, has sometimes overwhelmed foreign and local planners and decision makers. Relations with the International Monetary Fund and World Bank have had an on-again, off-again character, which have made it both difficult to follow and even more difficult to assess the impact of various policies.

After more than a decade of lesser arrangements with the IMF, the Government of the Republic of Zambia (GRZ) and the International Monetary Fund (IMF) agreed on a major package, to be started in 1983 but to intensify in 1985. In May 1987, following riots the previous December in the main towns of the Copperbelt, the Zambians suspended their participation and inaugurated their new Economic Recovery Programme, the NERP. From July 1987 through December 1988 the country's economy was supposed to follow an Interim National Development Plan (INDP) which was then superseded by the Fourth National Development Plan (FNDP) in January 1989, set to run for 5 years.

While planners worked over their documents and civil servants tried to incorporate the new objectives, heated debates ranged in Washington, Lusaka and elsewhere about Zambia's decision to service only a portion of their foreign debt (including those debts to the Bank and the Fund). Most donors decided to abandon Zambia to its fate.

After two years of "going it alone" the GRZ returned to the IMF for further talks in the spring of 1989. The focus was on how to restructure the mono-economy, on the context of growing debt arrears (estimated to be US$3.8 billion in March 1990) and declining social and physical infrastructure.

Widely differing interpretations are put forward of what such an economy should be trying to do and also what the various economic indicators really tell us. Zambia has proven to be anything but a shut-and-closed case for which structural reform has worked better, further complicated by the relatively brief periods for each of the strategies.

With the focus on macroeconomics, other aspects of Zambia's political and social nature have been overlooked, yet these are also crucial to the turnaround for the country. For example, 50 percent of Zambians live in and around its major cities and towns. This means that strategies based on agricultural production and the removal of subsidies for key consumer goods to the urban population is both limited in benefit and potentially explosive.

Equally, the ruling party – UNIP – has resorted to balancing the complicated ethnic mix of the country through reshuffling the deck of regional political key posts and generating enough employment through the civil service and parastatals. The Fund and the World Bank's suggestions to streamline the bureaucracy and cut recurrent expenditures hit at this political tactic (which has worked well for over 25 years) and also undermine the middle class elements in the urban areas.

Finally, the burdens that any form of structural adjustment requires fall unevenly in Zambian society – more heavily upon the poor and within that category, most heavily upon women and children. UNICEF and other agencies have acknowledged this tendency in most countries undergoing adjustment and have countered with calls for structural adjustment "with a human face." In the Zambian context, UNICEF, OXFAM (U.K.) and others have pointed to the alarming increase in nutrition-related child mortality as well as the long term effects of cutbacks in health and education.

This present volume consists of 3 parts, tracing the experiments of structural adjustment in Zambia. First is Roger Young's essay which covers the major elements of the Zambian economy and the early IMF programme (from 1983 to mid-1987). He outlines the main elements of the package as well as the problems that occurred from the rapid restructuring efforts in Zambia. The section concludes with the breakaway from the IMF's programme in mid-1987 and raises some questions for donors.

John Loxley's first section picks up from there, to follow the progress of the Zambian counter-structural adjustment, contained within the NERP. In order to analyze this strategy Professor Loxley explores the interim plan and its objectives as well as the FNDP plans and objectives and then looks at basic performance up to April 1989. The key problem of production on which he focuses is the centrality of copper mining to the whole economy and the present constrained state of that industry. Thus the mines were unable to take full advantage of the upswing in the copper prices from 1987 through mid-1989. Other undermining effects are the prevalence of the parallel (black) market, continuing inflation, an inability to reduce the deficit or raise expenditures on social services and the shortfall in the targets for increasing capacity utilization and employment.

On the more positive side, Loxley points to Zambia's increase in food production, to its achievements in slowly phasing out subsidies, to the rise in net foreign exchange and, finally, to the positive psychological effects of designing their own strategy rather than being dictated to by the Bank and the Fund.

The third part of this volume consists of an update by Loxley, tracing the key events from the summer of 1989, when negotiations between the Fund, Bank and GRZ were resumed, to mid-1990 when the Zambians entered a phase of "shadow structural adjustment." In such a phase, a country begins to introduce reforms which fit the orthodox IMF/World Bank conditions, as proof of its good intentions. However, these reforms are undertaken without external funding from the international financial institutions (IFIs) to cushion the economic and social impacts.

While these negotiations stretched on, physical and human conditions were deteriorating. Between January and November of 1989, prices increased by 122 percent. Fewer goods and services were available and basic commodities slowly became more expensive, as various subsidies were removed. Fourteen donor nations and eight international agencies in the Consultative Group for Zambia indicated that they would provide Zambia US$450 million to support the country's economic adjustment efforts in 1990 on condition that Zambia continued to make progress in implementing economic reforms and rescheduling some of the country's external debt. It was widely acknowledged that the intimidating proportions of Zambia's current debt would require the intervention of the Donor Group.

By June 1990 the pressure on the economy and people led to widespread rioting and demonstrations against these reforms and against the government. The unrest was capped by an attempted military coup in early July. These events point to the essential dilemma for a heavily indebted country that is trying to meet the conditions of the IFIs for readmittance to the international financial system, while facing a crumbling political consensus at home.

One feature which made these events particularly volatile was a new set of conditions attached to Zambia's reentry into the international system. These conditions are essentially political, and are characterized by international insistence that countries such as Zambia begin to move toward a multi-party system. President Kaunda publicly announced his willingness to hold a referendum on this point, although clearly stating his opposition to the movement away from rule by UNIP.

Discontent at the University of Zambia surfaced in May to June, with the key issues partly economic (the cost of food in the cafeterias) and partly political (support for multi-party system). When the price of mealie meal, the staple cereal, was suddenly hiked by 100 percent, the pot began to boil over. Rioting in Lusaka and Kafue (and, to a lesser degree, on the Copperbelt) was characterized by anti-regime activities as well as looting of food stores. These spontaneous activities ended when the police and army intervened, leaving 20 dead by late June 1990. After the abortive coup in July, there was a major reshuffling of military men in the top posts.

It would seem that the lessons of the "IMF riots" of the 1980s have been only partially understood at this time. For countries undergoing structural adjustment, the IFIs and donors are attempting to put together larger packages of funds which allow for more amelioration of social impact while the countries undergo major stresses. However, for those countries which have fallen behind in arrears, another set of rules applies which are extremely punitive. These countries, of which Zambia and also Guyana are examples, must undertake rigorous reforms – and show that they are sustaining them before the IFIs and donors will consider restarting their programmes. Financially this makes sense, as the IFIs are constrained by their rules of operation from engaging in work in countries which are in arrears. Meanwhile, the donors are often trying to put together funds to help repay those arrears and allow the country back into the system. But this kind of situation reflects more the rigidities and legalities of the international system than a thoughtful approach to the question of development for a debtor in arrears, such as Zambia.

For the longer term, one can hope that when the new structural adjustment package is finally agreed to, it will include considerable funds, either directly through the IFIs or through the donor community, to soften the blows of these policies for the most vulnerable members of these societies. These can take the shape of special feedings for children in schools and at clinics, weaning formula at very low cost, immunization vaccines, drugs for hospitals and clinics, basic supplies to schools, special food for pregnant and lactating mothers, etc. The possibilities are many and the needs pressing.

At this stage the full implications of the AIDs pandemic for Zambia are not clear, but the collapse of the health system is imminent and a rethinking of community-based palliative care would seem the only possible route. For the longer term redirection of the economy away from mining, the prospects for Zambia's manufacturing and semi-commercial agriculture are very controversial given the fact that most Fund and Bank programmes put strong emphasis on comparative advantage thinking.

Perhaps the entry of the UNDP into the debate will change donor thinking, reminding the international development community and especially the more economically-oriented IFIs that development must be seen as wider than merely economic growth. From their Human Development Report, 1990, they elaborate the philosophical point:

> ...the process of development should at least create a conducive environment for people, individually and collectively, to develop their full potential and to have a reasonable chance of leading productive and creative lives in accord with their needs and interests.

Ottawa, August 1990
Dr. Marcia Burdette

Part I

Adjusting to Poverty

1

The context
for
adjustment

Introduction

The colonial 'vision' of Zambia was that the territory, formerly known as Northern Rhodesia and richly endowed with copper and other minerals, would mine and export its wealth and, in return, become a net importer of agricultural and manufactured goods from the nearby African territories, or from the imperial home market, Britain. This perception that Zambia had only limited potential for agricultural or industrial development lingered for a long time after formal Independence was granted in 1964.

Current perceptions may conveniently, although simplistically, be divided into two: firstly, those who believe that independent Zambia proceeded to squander a potentially prosperous future based on this mineral wealth; and secondly, those who believe that Zambia represents a classic case of dependent and truncated development because of its overdependence on a single commodity export, itself a reflection of an economic structure which was inherited from a colonial past. In reality, the more accurate picture lies somewhere between these extremes.

As well, Zambia's economic development prospects cannot be divorced from the geopolitical circumstances of the region. Zambia's dependence goes well beyond a commodity dependence on copper; it includes a dependence on South Africa for imports, transport for Zambian exports and a vulnerability to South African military strength because of Zambia's opposition to the racist policies of the South African government.

The purpose of this report is to provide an analysis of recent macroeconomic trends in Zambia and the coherence and impact of attempts at economic policy reform. The paper focuses on the period 1980-87 with special attention being paid to the most recent effort to adjust to declining economic fortunes from October 1985 until May 1987 when Zambia abandoned the stewardship of IBRD and IMF structural adjustment programs and chose to seek an accommodation to economic decline by undertaking to meet its economic development objectives from its own resources.

The research for this report was commissioned by the Anglophone Africa branch of CIDA and was carried out by Professor John Loxley and John Baffoe, a graduate student, both of whom are at the University of Manitoba and who undertook field work in Zambia in September/October 1987 and by Roger Young of the North-South Institute who conducted an extensive documentary review and drafted this portion of the report.

The macroeconomic context

External factors

The Zambian economy has suffered an unprecedented decline in the period from the mid-1970s to mid-1987. Economic stagnation has characterized most of this period, with recurring and adverse external shocks compounded by domestic economic errors being the main reasons for the decline. The principal proximate cause of the decline has been the collapse in the export price of copper which began in the late 1960s, recovered for a period in the early 1970s, and then the downward trend recurred in the mid-1970s as a result of declining world demand for the natural product and the increasing use of substitutes such as aluminum. (Copper prices firmed dramatically in 1987, doubling in nominal terms in the eight months before the end of the year.)

The collapse in Zambia's terms of trade has been dramatic and at times compressed into intolerably short periods of time. The commodity terms of trade had fallen more than 77 percent between 1973 and 1984, including 50 percent between 1973 and 1975 and a further 55 percent from that level between 1976 and 1981 (see "Terms of Trade and Exchange Rate" graph). The terms of trade declined by

Zambia: Terms of Trade and Exchange Rate, 1965-84
1973=100

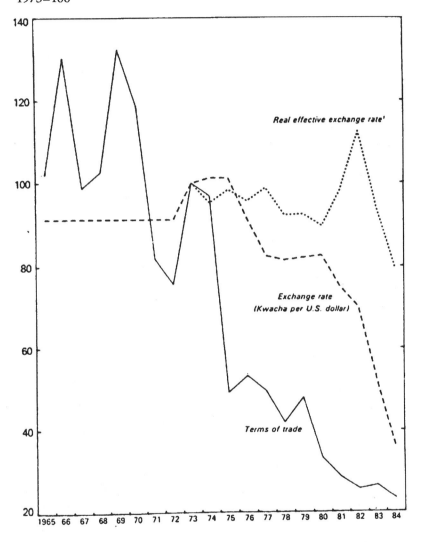

Real effective exchange rate[1]

Exchange rate
(Kwacha per U.S. dollar)

Terms of trade

[1]Series begins in 1973.

Sources: IMF, International Financial Statistics, "Zambia: Recent Economic Developments" (June 1984) and staff estimates.

a further 40 percent between 1980 and 1984. This reduction in the terms of trade led to a rapid decline in 'real imports' and a concomitantly rapid build-up of external debt. In volume terms, real imports fell by 30 percent between 1975 and 1980 but then fell an astounding two-thirds in the ensuing five years. This calamitous drop in imports was determined largely by declining copper prices. In value terms, real imports fell from US$1722 million in 1976 to US$700 million by 1985. Clearly there is an immense and pervasive shortage of foreign exchange which has taken hold over the economy (World Bank, 1986a, p.111). This 'structural' shortage of foreign exchange and thus, imports, continues to constrain Zambia's ability to grow, and to accomplish the structural adjustment objectives of the government and the international financial community which is trying to assist Zambia to achieve those objectives.

The fall in copper prices to the end of 1986 had been accompanied by a fall in copper production and export volume. Copper exports fell from a level of 700,000 tons in 1972 to 435,000 tons in 1986. Real prices for copper fell by 60 percent over this period. (There remains some disagreement as to the actual level of exports in recent years and as to the near-term prospects for copper production, exports, and prices. In late 1987, copper prices firmed substantially and production cost reductions together with the completion of the Copper Tailings Leach Plant 111 have given Zambia Consolidated Copper Mines Limited (ZCCM) reason to believe that 470,000 to 500,000 tons is an attainable and sustainable level of exports by the end of the decade.)

In addition to these contractionary trends, there was a rapid build-up of external indebtedness – rising from 40 percent of GDP in 1975 to 400 percent of GDP by the end of 1986 or an estimated US$5.7 billion. Even appreciating that this ratio tends to either under or overstate the extent of Zambia's indebtedness, depending on the exchange rate being employed, it is instructive to note that prior to any significant devaluation, at the end of 1985, external debt, including the undisbursed portion, had risen to 143 percent of GDP and scheduled debt servicing had risen to 43 percent of exports.

Official estimates in mid-1987 put Zambia's scheduled debt servicing, including principal, in 1987 at US$900 million, equivalent to 95 percent of estimated export earnings. Interest payments alone amount to US$339 million of which preferred multilateral creditors are due US$107 million, bilateral creditors US$105 million, and private creditors US$127 million. If arrears are included, then scheduled debt service rises to 150 percent of estimated export earnings. Both the level and terms of Zambia's debt are higher and harder than most other sub-Saharan African countries. Without more comprehensive debt relief, Zambia's prospects for real economic growth are highly remote. In May 1987, the government chose to limit debt servicing to 10 percent of exports after meeting essential payments for oil, for the mining industry through ZCCM, to International Air Transport Association (IATA) and for fertilizer. The profile of Zambia's debt at the end of 1986 is given in Table A.1.

Domestic policy performance

These negative external shocks and longer-term trends were accompanied by a series of domestic policy initiatives which served to compound their negative effects. The principal domestic policy areas to note include: an overvalued exchange rate regime; the real effective exchange rate (nominal exchange rate deflated by an index of relative rates of price inflation) rose some 30 percent between 1980 and 1982, even as Zambia's export earnings were falling. As copper prices were falling in real terms, so too should have the kwacha. That it did not is a reflection of government's view that the fall was temporary. Even when adjustment took place, the real effective exchange rate fell only 11 percent from its 1980 level by 1984, although the terms of trade had fallen 50 percent.

The overvalued exchange rate had turned the domestic terms of trade against agriculture and domestic food producers in particular. Intervention by government to allocate credit and foreign exchange was often on the basis of 'non-market' criteria and had led to increasingly administrative control and political criteria in the assessment of viable investment projects and the rationing of foreign exchange amongst competing needs and claims by private and public sector actors (World Bank, 1986a).

The government resorted to deficit financing in order to maintain consumption and investment in the economy as macroeconomic performance deteriorated. Viewing the negative external environment as one of temporary shocks, the government chose to finance, rather than adjust, to those events (World Bank, 1986a).

Macroeconomic impact

The domestic consequences of these negative external trends have been a prolonged fall in real incomes, consumption and savings. Real per capita income has fallen by 22 percent between 1978 and 1987. The data on real per capita incomes are given in Table 1. Net domestic investment, after allowing for the replacement costs of fixed capital, has been negative since 1979. Gross domestic savings have fallen from an already low level of 7.3 percent of GDP in 1979 to only 4.8 percent in 1985.

In an effort to maintain consumption levels in the face of declining external trends in the mid-1970s, the government's expenditure grew in real terms between 1977 and 1980, and the fiscal deficit reached 29 percent of GDP in 1980. Since 1983, there have been attempts to control the fiscal deficit through wage freezes on civil servants, staff reductions and reduced expenditures, particularly for consumption subsidies (see also Chapter 4 for a more detailed discussion of these points).

Government expenditure in recent years has been fuelled by debt-servicing obligations. However, revenues have not grown commensurately and the government deficit accounted for more than 15 percent of GDP in all years since 1980 except 1983 and 1984 when it was 9 percent. (World Bank, 1986a, p. 117.). In 1986, the deficit amounted to ZK2158 million, or approximately 20 percent of GDP, despite strict efforts at recurrent cost restraint.

There has been a rapid and continuing rise in the cost of living for the urban working class (a class of some importance to political stability in Zambia). Urbanization is much more pronounced in Zambia than the rest of sub-Saharan Africa. The all-items cost of living index for low-income individuals more than doubled between 1982 and 1985, and has risen an estimated 77 percent in 1986-87 (see Tables 3 and 8). The acute fall in real living standards for a basic wage earner has increased reliance on unofficial markets in order to obtain scarce basic consumer goods. The growth of parallel markets has put additional pressure on the government to improve economic performance.

The antecedents to policy reform

By the end of the 1970s, Zambia's economy was showing all the classic signs of deterioration and destabilization. There was increasing resort to IMF stabilization financing (described in the next chapter) throughout the latter 1970s and early 1980s. There was an increasing imbalance in the external account – the trade balance deteriorated from a positive level of US$96 million in 1976 to a negative value of US$436 million in 1981, a swing of US$500 million within just five years. (Admitting that 1976 was a very good year for commodity exporters such as Zambia does not diminish the magnitude, or the abruptness, of the downfall which subsequently befell countries such as Zambia.) In parallel, the current account balance also deteriorated between 1976 and 1981 by a sum of US$573 million (World Bank, 1986a, p. 105).

As a lower middle-income country, Zambia did not qualify automatically for large amounts of highly concessional financing during this period. Nevertheless, concessional bilateral and multilateral financing did rise nearly sixfold (in current dollars) from 1974-76 to 1979-81, but was insufficient to offset the full negative impact of external shocks and domestic policy errors. Zambia turned increasingly to private creditors and officially guaranteed credits to finance these growing external imbalances.

On the domestic side, the picture was equally bleak in retrospect. Government financing deteriorated rapidly, with the overall deficit accounting for 30 percent of GDP in fiscal year 1981. This required a significant amount of borrowing on foreign and domestic credit markets, particularly from the Bank of Zambia, in order to sustain the government's expenditure program. The causalities were the development budget, which was controlled more tightly than recurrent spending (which had to cope with higher subsidy payments as a result of poor agricultural performance), and domestic inflation, which accelerated rapidly from previous levels (see Table 3).

Even at this juncture in 1981 there was an emerging consensus that the external debt and its servicing requirements, together with rising inflation, was placing the government in an untenable position. There was increasing resort to the IMF for stabilization financing and the World Bank for capital projects which could not be sustained from domestic resources. Recourse to IMF financing which had risen significantly in 1977, ratcheted upwards again in 1981. IMF financing accumulated to US$856 million by the end of 1986, or some 15 percent of total outstanding debt. Non-concessional multilateral financing through the IBRD and concessional multilateral aid through the International Development Association (IDA) rose two and a half times in value while bilateral financing, although somewhat erratic, doubled in value in the five years after 1976.

The main parameters of Zambia's declining economic performance were thus set by 1981: poor economic growth due to declining terms of trade, driven principally by the fall in copper prices and demand; increasing governmental resort to international and domestic credit to finance rather than adjust to this change (which with hindsight was to become the main constraint on further growth); and increasing intervention by the government to unsuccessfully weigh against the declining standard of living for the vast majority of Zambians.

Yet in retrospect, 1981 must appear as a year of some optimism; there was positive growth in per capita income; food production was plentiful, with maize output surpassing levels not seen for four years, as producers responded to positive pricing incentives following a stabilization arrangement with the IMF that year.

Subsequent events through to 1985 were to prove to be much less propitious, and culminated in the government agreeing to a significant structural adjustment and policy reform program with the assistance, and at the urging, of the World Bank and the IMF. Policy reform began in 1983 and led to a comprehensive Economic Reform Program in September 1985.

In the period immediately before the reform program was agreed to, the economy approached collapse. Copper output continued to decline, and (with the exception of only 1982) had fallen to levels below those achieved in 1970.

In one respect, the fall in output was a blessing as the kwacha cost of production continued to escalate rapidly due to falling yields and ore quality. This was occurring even as world prices fell in dollar terms. The World Bank has noted that the mining industry suffers from substantial problems in addition to poor mineral ore quality and falling world prices, including labour unrest and a highly centralized management (World Bank, 1986a). There were large and growing losses sustained by ZCCM – by 1982, operating losses had grown to ZK140 million. In effect, the rest of the economy was subsidizing copper production, miners and the state as sole owner of the natural resource. The cruellest irony of all had befallen Zambia in that the very wealth that was to carry the nation to higher standards of living had become a massive wound, hemorrhaging wealth at a rate that the nation's policy makers could not believe, accept, or comprehend what to do.

The decline in the net value added from copper had the corresponding negative effect of contributing to Zambia's rising external indebtedness. The country's external indebtedness, defined as public and publicly guaranteed medium- and long-term debt rose 75 percent between 1980 and 1984. The rising external indebtedness was not accommodated without increasing distress; arrears accumulated at an alarming rate rising to a level of SDR 226 million by the end of 1983.

Commercial suppliers of credit stopped giving Zambia consideration after 1980 and net financial transfers were secured through reschedulings, some official debt relief, and a growing recourse to IMF resources with higher levels of policy conditionality being the price to be paid for this financing. Scheduled debt-service payments rose to 69 percent of the value of the export of goods and services in 1983, with actual debt servicing even after debt relief amounting to 42 percent of the value of exports in that year. The country then fell into a now familiar pattern of accumulating debt arrears, and having to make increasingly ad hoc decisions on whose debt to service, and seeking annual Paris Club reschedulings of official debt as could be cobbled together.

Domestic policies did little to encourage the confidence of national investors or food producers in the period up to 1985. Successive Fund stabilization programs called for increasing producer prices for maize, the basic consumption item in the low-income earners' budget. As Table 6.1 demonstrates, maize producer prices rose in real terms until 1985. Even though the domestic terms of trade moved toward food producers, the continuing and intensified inefficiencies in NAMBOARD, the state-owned buyer of domestic food crops, undermined whatever benefits might have accrued to producers from higher farmgate prices (K. Good, 1986). Maize production stagnated and by all accounts performed below potential during the period 1983-85. (Zambia now faces another period of food scarcity as drought is affecting output in certain regions of the country.) High and rising consumer subsidies, the result of rising producer prices alongside controlled consumer prices, contributed in a major way to the government's deficit financing and resultant inflationary pressures.

The upshot of these events was an economy in very serious condition by 1985. There was both an unsustainable domestic fiscal deficit and a severe external imbalance that had to be faced. There was no alternative to structural adjustment; the only remaining questions were how much could the economy bear and how long could its citizens tolerate the prevailing condition of deprivation. The initial answer was to be found in the Economic Reform Program (ERP) of September 1985.

Zambia's record debt burden

Zambia's external indebtedness has grown to unsustainably high levels, imperilling the country's import and growth potential and presenting its policy makers with an enormous challenge. The debt situation also poses some difficult challenges and problems for Zambia's external creditors.

Zambia's debt, at the end of 1986, was estimated by the World Bank at US$5709 million which is one of the highest debt loads relative to GDP in the developing world. At four times the estimated 1986 U.S. dollar GDP, Zambia's debt burden measured in these terms is higher than that of the major Third World debtors and higher than that of almost all other African debt-distressed nations. Zambia's scheduled debt-servicing ratio for 1987 is equal to 95 percent of estimated export earnings without any progress on accumulated arrears; including arrears boosts the debt servicing to 150 percent of exports. The ratio of debt to GDP must be treated with caution for all developing country debtors because the denominator, GDP, is arrived at by using official exchange rates. The rapid rise in this debt to GDP ratio in the Zambian case is a direct reflection of the devaluation of the kwacha from 1986.

The country's debt profile is presented in Table A.1. Debt owed to multilateral institutions, (e.g., IBRD, ADB) excluding the IMF, accounts for 17 percent of outstanding debt and 21 percent of outstanding long-term debt. The share of non-concessional, multilateral debt is high in Zambia's case although other African countries such as Ghana, Kenya and Liberia carry similar proportions. Multilateral institutions provided net financing of US$50 million to Zambia in 1986.

The IMF with US$856 million owing at the end of 1986, or 15 percent of all debt, represents a major creditor. In 1986, net payments to the Fund were approximately US$100 million and will continue to represent, in the short run, a significant obligation for Zambia. Preferred multilateral creditors, such as the IBRD, African Development Bank (ADB), and IMF, account for a third of Zambia's external obligations at the current time.

Bilateral creditors hold the largest share of Zambia's debt at 40 percent or US$2.2 billion. Most bilateral credit is extended on concessional but not very generous terms – the grant element of outstanding bilateral credits is 35 percent – which is low by African standards. Development Assistance Committee (DAC) countries account for 70 percent of bilateral claims. There is one element to note however; only one-quarter of Zambia's bilateral debt is denominated in U.S. dollars. For example, the debt of both West Germany (US$378 million) and Japan (US$281 million) is appreciating against the U.S. dollar as all this debt is denominated in deutsche marks and yen respectively.

Canada has provided all of its bilateral assistance to Zambia on a grant basis since 1986 and recently announced its intention to convert outstanding CIDA loans already disbursed on a highly concessional basis (0-10-40) to grants (Cdn$80 million approximately).

Most DAC debt, and servicing obligations on interest and principal, is being rescheduled and payments due in 1987 will either be rescheduled or added to arrears. But the interest rate on reschedulings and arrears is at commercial rates and, therefore, outstanding debt continues to rise at the rate of interest, approximately 8.6 percent in 1986.

Private creditors account for 13 percent of all long-term debt. This comprises both banks (60 percent) and suppliers with one-third of bank debt carrying official guarantees. Some of this officially backed private debt has been rescheduled at recent Paris Club meetings leaving an estimated 8 percent of Zambia's debt as private, long-term debt. This represents Zambia's most expensive debt. Zambia has not kept current in its payments to private creditors in the past, allowing these to be added to arrears. Arrears to private creditors are now equal to 37 percent of all arrears. Private creditors did make net transfers to Zambia in 1986 (US$16 million) all of which went to ZCCM.

It is Zambia's short-term private debt which has increased most rapidly in recent times, nearly doubling between 1980 and 1986. This debt now comprises 19 percent of all Zambia's debt. This consists of import financing, arrears on letters of credit, bridge loans to the Central Bank and letters of credit with foreign banks.

Debt rescheduling for Zambia under Paris Club arrangements has been relatively generous in that interest and previously rescheduled principal are also being rescheduled but, as noted, no concessions are being given on the interest rate on rescheduled debt.

And yet in the short term, that is, the next five years, Zambia's debt-servicing ratio will remain well above levels consistent with either growth in income or imports. One official estimate prepared in mid-1987 stated that Zambia will require an additional US$1150 million between 1988 and 1993 (or $230 million per year), in addition to debt relief provided by more generous Paris Club reschedulings, to reduce debt servicing to 25 percent, the target level which the World Bank has estimated is reasonable for low-income debt-distressed countries (World Bank, 1987c). This external financing target assumes that there is no relief provided by preferred creditors.

Beyond this level of financing, it is estimated that an additional US$225-250 million per year will be required to finance a negative resource balance in order to ensure modest growth in real per capita income of 1 percent per annum. These projections were based on an assumption that Zambia would continue an IMF structural adjustment program. This assumption must now be questioned in light of the government's commitment to pursue an alternative set of policies. These projections would also have to be modified should world copper prices remain at current levels of £1600 per ton for any period of time.

Securing an extra US$450 million annually in external financing seems highly unlikely under current international financial institutional arrangements and bilateral donor country aid spending restraints. (One would have to assume that fully US$1000 per ton of the increased price of copper in 1987 would have been net foreign exchange to the Zambian economy and that these price levels will be maintained in real terms over the next five years to expect additional external financing on the scale suggested above should Zambia not undertake a new structural adjustment effort consistent with Fund and Bank criteria and analysis).

As part of its 'New Economic Recovery Program' announced in May 1987, the government of Zambia stated its intention to limit debt-service payments to 10 percent of export earnings net of strategic payments for oil and fertilizers and to ZCCM and IATA.

The government has estimated that after these strategic payments are made, some US$20-30 million will be available for debt servicing. By early 1988, the government was US$80 million in arrears to the World Bank and as at September 30, 1987, SDR 291 million (approximately US$380 million) in arrears to the IMF. The IMF has declared Zambia ineligible to use the general resources of the Fund. The government is not making any payments currently to its preferred creditors and is hoping that new net financing from bilateral sources will offset the loss of net transfers from multilateral sources. If one assumes no immediate drop in net bilateral financing, then Zambia will have to replace approximately US$50 million in new net financing that will not be available in 1987 from multilateral agencies whose debt is not being serviced. By December 1987, several Nordic donors had agreed to finance a substantial portion of these arrears owed to the World Bank on condition that Zambia meet the rest and all future obligations (*Financial Times*, December 3,1987).

Japan and the European Community (EC) have recently announced additional, non-conditional, balance of payments assistance to Zambia. Japan has committed US$20 million. This will go a significant way toward replacing lost net multilateral finance.

Higher copper prices, of course, are more important for total foreign exchange but the medium- and longer-term outlook is uncertain. With the declaration by the government not to service IMF obligations, and given that Zambia was making net repayments to the Fund, total available foreign exchange in the short run will be enhanced. The prospects for the longer term are more uncertain, however. In late 1987, the government of Zambia and the World Bank initiated new discussions aimed at reconstituting a structural adjustment program and at unlocking the flow of external funds (*Financial Times*, December 3,1987).

Table A.1
Zambia's Debt Profile (Year End 1986, US$ million)

Source	Balance Outstanding	%	Principal Payments	%	Interest Payments	%
World Bank	460	8	30.0	5	36.5	11
IDA	191	3	0.0	0	2.3	1
Other	305	5	32.8	6	21.0	6
Total Multilateral	**956**	**17**	**62.8**	**11**	**59.8**	**18**
IMF	856	15	220.9	40	47.5	14
Total Preferred	**1812**	**32**	**283.8**	**51**	**107.3**	**32**
Export Credits	1024	18	114.5	20	70.1	21
ECA Debt	117	2	42.4	8	9.8	3
ODA	1131	20	37.0	7	25.3	7
Total Bilateral	**2272**	**40**	**193.9**	**35**	**105.1**	**31**
Financial Institutions	265	5	14.3	3	12.1	4
Suppliers' Credits	268	5	66.7	12	16.8	5
Short-term Debt	1091	19	_[a]	0	88.2	20
Total Private[b]	**1625**	**28**	**81.0**	**15**	**127.1**	**37**
Total Debt	**5709**		**558.6**		**339.5**	

[a] Assumes short-term debt is rolled over.
[b] A small portion of suppliers' credits are officially guaranteed.
Source: World Bank 1987c.

2

Structural adjustment and policy reform

Introduction

The structural adjustment and economic reform program of October 1985 unilaterally ended by the Zambian government in May 1987 is perhaps the best known and most controversial of Zambia's attempts to cope with structural disequilibrium in both its domestic and external accounts. In fact, though, Zambia has been a 'ward' of the IMF for some time, the latest effort simply reflects the fact that in 1985, Zambia was brought into the intensive care ward after having been an outpatient on and off for the past 10 years.

Zambia had by 1987 become a prolonged user of Fund financing on an increasingly more conditional basis. This chapter is a brief overview of Fund programs in Zambia with an emphasis upon the most recent arrangement. A synopsis of Fund arrangements with Zambia and macroeconomic performance criteria and actual results is presented in an Appendix to this chapter. A more complete treatment of the Fund's programs in Zambia can be found in Ndulo and Sakala, 1987.

Zambia's earliest dealings with the Fund, beginning in 1972, were seen as routine. The drop in world copper prices and the simultaneous fall in Zambian production which began in the early 1970s, was compounded by the first oil shock and a rapid deterioration in the balance of payments. In many respects, Zambia was just one of very many LDCs suffering similar difficulties and, as a middle-income country, it was not perceived as deserving of special attention.

Early Fund arrangements exhibited low conditionality relative to the latter period. The government also appeared to have a fairly benign view that external shocks were of a temporary nature with which it could cope by reducing domestic absorption, largely by restraining government expenditure, and finally, by financing balance of payments deficits until copper prices and export volume steadied. It took some time to appreciate that diversification away from copper was required to reduce the structural decline in the terms of trade and that this would be necessary in order to achieve any sustainable adjustment to external shocks, enhance the prospects for exports to grow and move the economy into a position of more sustainable growth.

By 1983, there was widespread recognition that the external shocks were not temporary but were more likely to recur and not to be easily reversible; that copper prices would not recover quickly and that domestic copper deposits were deteriorating in quality and quantity. And yet this was the precise time that external capital flows from all sources fell dramatically, compounding an already very precarious situation. As shown in Table 7, external loans fell by 60 percent between 1980 and 1984. While multilateral lending fell only 3.4 percent over this period, bilateral lending fell 59 percent and private credits a full 85 percent.

By 1985, the continued deterioration of the external sector, both weak exports and rapidly falling imports, together with a growing appreciation that there was an unsustainable external payments position, led to a recognition that comprehensive reform was in order.

IMF arrangements with Zambia: 1973-87
An overview

1973

A one year Stand-by Arrangement of SDR 19 million was negotiated in light of a rapid fall in copper output and prices which had led to a fall in foreign exchange and gross international reserves and government revenue. Low conditional first tranche drawing with requirement to reduce domestic absorption was undertaken.

1976-77

Another one year Stand-by Arrangement of SDR 19 million was negotiated after terms of trade continued to deteriorate and the government budget deficit rose. Greater conditionality with actions to remove consumption subsidies, reduce domestic absorption through a wage freeze, and diversify exports was imposed. Falling terms of trade, together with the intensified conflict with Rhodesia undermined the program's objectives for economic growth and the government's fiscal deficit. GDP fell nearly 5 percent in 1977; inflation doubled to 20 percent and overall balance of payments deficit rose to SDR 243 million against a projected level of SDR 65 million. The program was unable either to arrest the decline in GDP or to restore a momentum toward balance of payments equilibrium.

1978-80

A two year Stand-by Arrangement for SDR 250 million, equivalent to 177 percent of quota came into operation. The stand-by was supported by nearly SDR 70 million in CFF and Trust Fund financing. The objectives were to reduce domestic absorption and move to equilibrium in the balance of payments. The kwacha was devalued 10 percent and Zambia was required to eliminate arrears on external credit. More rigorous quantitative targets were imposed to constrain expansion of domestic credit, freeze wages, rationalize copper production and raise agricultural producer prices.

Most program criteria were met. There was improvement in the costs of production of copper, and export prices rose. There was lower inflation and the balance of payments did improve, but a severe drought hurt food production leading to food imports and a new foreign exchange crisis by 1980 as higher oil import prices were affecting the trade balance. Uneven economic growth derived from the movements in copper prices. Imports were constrained leading to underutilization of productive capacity.

1980-83

A three year Extended Fund Facility (EFF) for SDR 800 million or 378 percent of quota, with the objective of a more comprehensive structural adjustment to external and internal imbalances was made available. Approved in May 1981, there was agreement to restrain expenditure and redirect government financing toward the agricultural sector, to reform fiscal and monetary policy, control domestic credit expansion, decrease copper production costs and increase output, review exchange rate policy and foreign exchange management and take action to eliminate arrears. Copper prices and output declined leading to a renewal of the pressures, and the lack of progress in clearing arrears and containing domestic credit expansion, which rose quickly in response to agricultural credit demand associated with a bumper harvest, led to the EFF being cancelled in July 1982.

1983-84

A one year Stand-by Arrangement for SDR 211 million was arranged so as to restore the financial stability of the economy after falling mineral prices led to further deterioration of the balance of payments and larger losses by parastatals which were financed through the domestic banking system.

There were conventional reductions in domestic expenditures through freezes on civil service wages and employment, and added incentives for food producers and manufactures exporters through price decontrol. In January 1983, the kwacha was devalued 20 percent and delinked from SDR in July 1983. Foreign debt-service payments due in 1983 were rescheduled, but Zambia fell even further behind as copper exports and prices performed poorly. The Stand-by was suspended in December 1983 with SDR 45 million not drawn when disagreement arose between the government and the Fund over arrears and the domestic budget.

1984-86

The twenty-one-month Stand-by Arrangement for SDR 225 million had as its objectives once again progress toward stabilization of external and internal balances. The flexible exchange rate policy of 1983 and expenditure restraint were continued. A new policy element to promote non-traditional exports was the retention of 50 percent of foreign exchange.

There were measures to deal with rescheduling and arrears but performance targets on arrears were not met. GDP growth stagnated and inflation rose while budget deficit rose too as copper prices fell and Zambia faced high debt-servicing costs.

The IMF agreed to a waiver in September 1984 to allow a purchase of SDR 80 million. There were further negotiations on foreign exchange crisis but no further drawings were made in 1985 and facility was cancelled in February 1986.

Given the deterioration in the terms of trade, the rising debt-servicing burden (the scheduled debt-servicing ratio rose from 31 percent in 1980 to 70 percent in 1984), and the acute shortage of foreign exchange available for imports, a foreign exchange auction was introduced in October 1985, allowing market forces to determine exchange rate and final uses of foreign exchange. (See pages 30-34 for fuller discussion.) Complementary policies to liberalize trade and financial payments, and to decontrol interest rates were also undertaken. Initial auctions allocated US$5 million rising to US$9 million by February 1986 when oil, IATA, Tanzania-Zambia Oil Pipeline (TAZAMA), and Tanzania-Zambia Railway (TAZARA) payments were included in the auction. The Zambian kwacha fell from ZK2.22 to the dollar in October 1985 to ZK8.07 to the dollar in October 1986 and then fell to ZK15.25 to the dollar in December 1986. Excess demand for imports and growing uncertainty had driven the rate down.

The initial experience with the implementation of the auction was reasonably successful with ZCCM and the private sector, particularly manufacturers, being the principal beneficiaries. There was a generally disappointing take-up of foreign exchange by the agricultural sector due to an overall lack of liquidity resulting from low prices in the past. For details on the purchasers of foreign exchange, see "IMF and the Zambian Economy" (Ncube et al, 1987.)

1986

A two year Stand-by Arrangement for SDR 229 million was negotiated in November 1986, to sustain the reform program and structural adjustment effort of the government. This was abandoned in May 1987 when the Zambian government fixed the exchange rate at ZK8 to the dollar, limited debt servicing to 10 percent of exports and reintroduced price controls for basic consumer goods, especially maize meal. Earlier attempts at decontrol of maize prices in December 1986 had led to riots in the major urban centres, which threatened the survival of the incumbent government.

(Tables A.2.1 through A.2.6 are taken from Ndulo and Sakala, 1987.)

Table A2.1
Financial Flows Between Zambia and IMF: 1971-84
(million kwacha)[a]

Year	Repurchase	CCF	Oil Facility	Use of IMF Credit Credit Tranche	Extended Facility	Total
1971	–	14.7				14.7
1972	29.5	29.5				
1973	29.5	14.7	44.2			
1974	29.9	15.0	44.9			
1975	28.6	28.6	14.2	14.3	57.2	
1976	17.5	35.0	27.4	25.4	87.8	
1977	17.5	52.5	27.4	7.8	87.8	
1978	–	108.4	30.4	111.1	251.0	
1979	26.9	95.5	24.2	205.8	327.8	
1980	45.1	69.7	16.6	227.3	315.8	
1981	48.4	98.2	9.0	228.5	307.3	643.0
1982	88.3	108.1	1.4	172.8	307.3	589.6
1983	146.0	243.9	–	185.9	384.1	814.0
1984		410.9	–	510.1	614.8	1,535.8

[a] Converted at SDR exchange rate.
OL – Oil facility; CR – Credit tranche; EF – Extended facility.
Source: *IMF International Financial Statistics 1984.*

Table A2.2
Performance Criteria: 1976-77 Facility

	1976 Criteria	Out-turn	1977 Out-turn
		(Annual rates of change)	
Real GDP	1.0	4.3	-4.3
Consumer Prices	10.15	18.9	19.6
Domestic Credit	16.9	26.9	30.0
Broad Money	11.0	26.5	12.1
Government Budget			
Revenue and Grants	0.9	-0.3	10.8
Total Expenditure	-13.1	5.9	2.0
Currency Adjustment			
Nominal	-20.0	-20.0	–
Real Effective Rate	–	-2.8	3.3
		(Percent of GDP)	
Budget Deficit	8.5	14.0	12.7
Domestic Bank Financing	3.1	12.3	11.3
Foreign Financing	3.8	1.6	0.9
Current Account Balance	-9.6	-5.08	-9.0
		(millions of SDRs)	
Overall Balance of Payment	-65	-165	-243
Payments Arrears	70	203	393
		(US cents per pound)	
LME Copper Price	65.0	63.6	59.4

Source: Bank of Zambia.

Table A2.3
Performance Criteria: 1978-80 Facility

	1978 Criteria	1978 Out-turn	1979 Criteria	1979 Out-turn
Real GDP	-2.0 – 3.0	3.9	1.0 – 2.0	-7.7
Consumer Prices	16 – 18	16.4	10.0	9.68
Domestic Credit	18.2	17.4	8.8	9.3
Broad Money	13.5	-8.5	21.2	30.2
Current Budget				
Revenue and Grants	11.5	15.5	-1.0	7.8
Total Expenditure	-3.7	-8.4	-1.4	49.5
Terms of Trade	8.0	-14.1	4.9	13.6
Currency Adjustment				
Nominal	-10.0	-10.0	–	–
Real Effective Rate	–	-7.6	–	-0.1
	(Percent of GDP)			
Budget Deficit	7.6	7.3	7.0	13.7
Domestic Bank Financing	4.3	4.2	1.9	2.3
Foreign Financing	2.6	0.9	5.0	5.4
Current Account Balance	9.2	-10.1	-2.0	1.4
	(millions of SDRs)			
Overall Balance of Payment	-140	-207	–	173
Payments Arrears	397	495	422	350
	(US cents per pound)			
LME Copper Price	60.0	61.9	70.0	89.5

Source: Bank of Zambia.

Table A2.4
Performance Criteria: 1981-83 Facility[a]

	1981 Criteria	Out-turn	1982 Forecast
Real GDP	5.0	4.7	5.0
Consumer Prices	14 – 16	14.0	12–14
Domestic Credit	14.7	46.7	–
Broad Money	13.1	7.9	–
Interest Rates			
Maximum Lending Rates	12.0	12.0	12.0
Nominals	-2 to -4	-2.0	-2 to -0
Government Budget			
Revenue and Grants	12.4	5.4	13.0
Total Expenditure	-12.3	-21.1	8.8
Terms of Trade	14.0	-14.2	14
	(Percent of GDP)		
Budget Deficit	7.1	14.0	5.5
Domestic Bank Financing	4.1	5.4	2.2
Foreign Financing	2.0	8.1	2.2
Current Account Balance	-9.8	16.3	-5.6
	(millions of SDRs)		
Overall Balance of Payment	-152	-327	-35
Payments Arrears	339	501	211
	(US cents per pound)		
LME Copper Price	93.0	79.0	115.0

[a]The 1981-83 facility became inoperative after 1981 and was cancelled in July 1982. The 1982 data reflect targets established at the start of the facility in 1981.
Source: Bank of Zambia.

Table A2.5
Performance Criteria: 1983-84 Facility

	1983 Criteria	Out-turn
	(Annual rates of change)	
Real GDP	–	1.8
Consumer Prices	25 – 23	19.7
Domestic Credit	10.7	8.4
Broad Money	12.5	11.1
Interest Rates		
Maximum Lending Rate		
Nominal	13.0	13.0
Real	-12 to -17	-6.6
Government Budget		
Revenue and Grants	26.8	19.5
Total Expenditure	-10.0	-16.4
Terms of Trade	2.7	3.5
Currency Adjustment		
Nominal	-34.8	-38.5
Real Effective Rate	–	-18.4
	(Percent of GDP)	
Budget Deficit	5.6	6.3
Domestic Bank Financing	3.7	2.7
Foreign Financing	0.5	1.8
Current Account Balance	-7.4	-8.3
	(millions of SDRs)	
Overall Balance of Payment	-100	-89.6
Payments Arrears	720	720
	(US cents per pound)	
LME Copper Price	76.0	72.2

Source: Bank of Zambia.

Table A2.6
Performance Criteria: 1984-86 Facility[a]

	1984 Criteria	Out-turn
	(Annual rates of change)	
Real GDP	–	-2.7
Consumer Prices	25.0	20.0
Domestic Credit	11.1	11.1
Broad Money	12.0	18.0
Interest Rates		
Maximum Lending Rate		
Nominal	17.0	17.0
Real	-8.0	-3.0
Government Budget		
Revenue and Grants	15.0	8.6
Total Expenditure	12.8	17.5
Terms of Trade	-11.9	-12.9
Currency Adjustment		
Nominal	-30.0	-31.3
Real Effective Rate	–	-14.4
	(Percent of GDP)	
Budget Deficit	4.5	10.7
Domestic Bank Financing	3.3	4.0
Foreign Financing	1.8	1.3
Current Account Balance	10.7	8.2
	(millions of SDRs)	
Overall Balance of Payment	-93	-66.3
Payments Arrears	620	718
	(US cents per pound)	
LME Copper Price	65	62.5

[a]The facility became inactive in April 1985 and was cancelled in February 1986.
Source: Bank of Zambia.

3

How to assess
the impact of SAP

When macroeconomic imbalances have been allowed to persist for a long time, as has been the case in Zambia over much of the past seven years, it is necessary that some structural adjustment take place in order to bring the economy back toward stability in the basic external and internal balances.

External stabilization under structural adjustment programs normally will require an exchange rate devaluation to increase the local currency value of tradeable goods. In theory, small open economies such as Zambia will increase their export earnings and reduce import costs by devaluing their currencies.

There is a strong presumption that import-substituting production will respond flexibly to the new incentive structure and that import demand will fall in response to higher import prices. However, increasing evidence suggests that structural bottlenecks may well restrict efficient import substitution in the short to medium term. Given the import intensity of African manufacturing, demand is likely to be quite price inelastic in the short term and will require supply enhancing policy instruments too (Green, 1986).

Internal imbalance in the context of current SAP programs is most often believed to occur when domestic demand exceeds domestic supply, leading to price inflation and/or increased non-market allocation of goods and services. However, increasingly, it is recognized, that in the context of low-income African economies, supply-enhancing policies are badly needed when per person consumption is falling and basic human needs remain so inadequately met. There may be chronic shortages of foreign exchange – certainly true in the case of Zambia – which result in scarcities of intermediate inputs, spare parts, etc. – all of which can lead to high prices.

There is also the theoretical expectation that under conditions of increasing scarcity of basic goods, especially if these shortages are prolonged, parallel market exchanges will increase as goods may not be available through official channels. This can lead to rising prices and further rationing of goods beyond the reach of the poorest. There is also the possibility of increased political unrest.

The practicality of this macroeconomic orthodoxy, however, may well be limited in the case of poor countries by the often intolerable costs that must be borne by the society in order to achieve stabilization. It is usual to find that stabilization programs require demand depression to reduce domestic absorption of resources as well as to reduce imports in the short run. Thus, it is often political resistance that leaves governments fighting against stabilization programs unless there is some evidence of economic growth in the short term to ameliorate the economic, social and political costs of stabilization.

This resistance is likely to originate with those whose interests are being most directly and adversely affected by the stabilization policies. Given that the poorest are unlikely to have a strong political voice, it is quite probable that their interests could be overlooked during the SAP program, unless particular attention is given to their needs and circumstances.

With the growing recognition that SAP programs, in view of their orthodox prescription of initially reducing domestic demand, will lead to a fall in consumption for the poor, there has been renewed interest in reducing the social costs of adjustment for the poorest. Even as and when growth is restored, there is reason to ask whether the poor will share proportionately in a growing economy (UNICEF, 1987, and Development Committee, 1987).

At a theoretical level, it is possible to identify the likely winners and losers of a SAP process. Devaluation, one of the key elements of a SAP, will benefit producers of tradeable goods especially exporters and efficient producers of import substitutes, as net domestic currency export prices and import prices increase. The expectation in the Zambian context is that the mining sector, agricultural producers, both of domestic food and export, and efficient producers of import substitutes will be the net beneficiaries of devaluation as domestic currency export prices and food import prices rise. There is a strong presumption in the general theoretical literature that these producers will be among the upper 40 percent of income earners in society.

   *   Decontrolling domestic prices will lead to increases in the prices of basic consumption goods, of which food will be of particular concern to the urban poor. The direct beneficiary will be the domestic public sector budget while consumers in general will lose, with the degree of their losses being dependent on the price and availability of food prior to the price decontrol situation. In Zambia, it was precisely urban-based and poor consumers who led the rioting in December 1986 and contributed to the abandonment of the SAP by the government.

   *   Reduced domestic expenditure will often have to be accommodated in the African case by the public sector through lower expenditures, layoffs, reduced financial transfers to parastatals and, thus, layoffs there too. The consequences, especially in economies such as Zambia with strong structural rigidities, will be lower levels of consumption for those losing employment; these reduced consumption levels may persist for a long period of time as new employment opportunities are slow to materialize. The resulting welfare losses may well be significant and require special attention. Recent work by UNICEF (1987) has also demonstrated that the impact of government restraint may fall disproportionately on the poor as access to schools, health facilities, and food subsidies is curtailed. (It is important in assessing the impact of SAP programs to know of the availability and access to these services by the poor in the pre-SAP period to be able to judge the impact of SAP itself. This is a data requirement that is, however, most often impossible to fulfill in practice.)

The actual impact of SAP programs requires detailed information disaggregating the poor and the differential consequences of adjustment programs on their consumption, the prices which they face for basic consumption goods, changes in their real incomes, and their access to "basic needs goods and services." Chapter 4 is an attempt to provide a partial assessment of the impact of recession and 'failed' adjustment in the Zambian context.

There are a number of conceptual approaches to assessing the efficacy of structural adjustment programs, and their relative appropriateness will depend on the purpose and context of the assessment which is being undertaken (Loxley, 1986 and 1987). In this study we will focus on evaluating the performance of the Zambian economy during the reform program and relative to the specific targets set out at the beginning of the program.

There are a number of points which must be borne in mind as one attempts to assess the impact of the reform program in the Zambian context. The first is that the structural adjustment program, to which the Zambian government agreed in 1983 and which the IMF and World Bank assisted with program financing, did not endure long enough to allow a realistic assessment of its performance relative to an ex-ante situation. The adjustment program was initially centred on stabilization goals and only in October 1985 did a more fundamental reform occur. Given the deterioration in the country's external sector-declining terms of trade and rising arrears on external debt, together with a large and persistent fiscal deficit, the immediate goals of the reform program were stabilization. This stabilization program contained elements that were designed to promote greater economic efficiency and thus return the economy to growth. However, the more comprehensive policy reform aimed at structural adjustment was substantially abandoned as early as December 1986, some 13 months after the program was begun (when rioting erupted in Zambia's major urban centres, 15 persons were killed, and there was the largest demonstration of disaffection since Independence).

The Zambian government formally abandoned the structural adjustment program in May, 1987, when it reimposed a fixed rate for foreign exchange; set a limitation on external debt servicing; ended the liberalization of prices for basic consumer goods by reimposing price controls; and abandoned the policy of wage freezes and restraint, and demand compression through restrictions on increases in government expenditure. In July 1987, the government announced its intent to pursue quite a different course under an Interim National Development Plan (INDP).

4

Assessing the impact of the economic reform program 1985-86

The stabilization and subsequent adjustment program which the government agreed to undertake can be dated from 1983 but was focused on structural adjustment in the period from October 1985. It had a number of elements to it including the following policy changes and initiatives.

- An effective real devaluation of the exchange rate was to be maintained through the implementation of a foreign exchange auctioning system.

- An effective real devaluation would serve to encourage 'nontraditional exports' in the agricultural and manufacturing sectors as the exchange rate fell, and to boost foreign exchange earnings. As well as diversifying away from copper, devaluation would serve to enhance the kwacha earnings of ZCCM.

- The removal of public sector financed consumer subsidies, particularly for processed maize meal, which accounted for 15 percent of total government expenditure prior to the reform.

- Further public sector expenditure restraint through enhanced controls on recurrent costs consisted primarily of a wage freeze for civil servants, and reforms to revenue collection to enhance public sector income. The ultimate objective was to move toward domestic fiscal balance.

- New incentives were offered to attract foreign and domestic private investment, especially for export.

- Decontrolled parastatal pricing was initiated to permit these enterprises to reduce their own fiscal deficits and their charge on the Central Bank.
- Complementing the foreign exchange auction system, there was a decontrolling of interest rates by the government through an auctioning of Treasury Bill notes as the principal instrument for controlling changes in the money supply. Previously, the government had relied on its overdraft facility with the Bank of Zambia to finance its expenditures.

Performance under the recovery program

We will assess the Economic Reform Program against its major objectives, given the caveat noted in the preceding chapter concerning the duration and intensity of the program. The main performance criteria for assessing the structural adjustment then are:

- restore economic growth,
- increase foreign exchange earnings and export diversification via devaluation, and
- control inflation through a reduction in government expenditure to be achieved by a combination of a wage freeze and civil service staff reductions; via lower subsidies for consumption goods. Inflation was also to be controlled by greater fiscal and monetary discipline more generally.

Economic growth

The economy had stagnated prior to the ERP and while there was some improvement in aggregate growth performance in 1983-84 and 1984-85 and into 1986, this was quite modest and per person levels of income and consumption continued to deteriorate. From Table 1 it is clear that the rapid fall in living standards was not arrested during the reform period. The rate at which income and consumption levels were falling did slow during 1983-87 but imperceptibly so. The most dramatic fall in income preceded the ERP but the ERP was expected to increase per capita consumption and it failed to do so by itself. Therefore, it is not surprising that public and governmental support for the program collapsed.

Wage and salary earners were among the hardest hit after 1983 as the data in Tables 1, and 8 demonstrate. 'Adjustment theory' suggests that income should be transferred to producers of tradeables under a structural adjustment. In the case of Zambia, this should have translated into gains for the mining and agricultural sectors. But for some of those in the mining sector, the income losses were staggering with middle-grade mine workers suffering particularly between 1981 and 1986 when fully 84 percent of real income was lost. It should be noted that all groups suffered losses prior to the ERP too, so that these real income and consumption losses cannot be wholly and casually attributed just to the reform program.

Value added in agriculture registered an 11 percent increase from 1981 to 1986, although this represents a fall in real per capita value added in agriculture too. The reform did contribute to maintaining the domestic terms of trade vis-a-vis agriculture and the rest of the economy. The real producer price for maize fell only marginally in a situation where inflation was rising over this period. It fluctuated from an index level of 115 to 109 between 1980 and 1985. However, production responses after 1981 to these pricing incentives were relatively weak and fluctuated around 1978-80 levels on average. As a result, agriculture's share of GDP has changed only marginally in the past two decades. Some of the weakness in agriculture is attributable to drought conditions during 1981-82, but it is also a result of ineffective and inefficient input provision, procurement and marketing by the state (see K. Good, 1986). The country's transportation infrastructure has also deteriorated and this too contributes to a weak performance by the agricultural sector. With the emergence of poor weather conditions in 1987, there is a danger of widening malnutrition in Zambia.

With the implementation of the Economic Reform Program, and in particular, the real devaluation of the kwacha, the mining industry improved its performance considerably. The kwacha price for copper rose dramatically and operating losses were reduced. By the end of ZCCM's first quarter operating report for June 30, 1987, the company had recorded positive earnings. By mid-1987, world prices were firming and by the fourth quarter had risen significantly to £1500 per metric ton against a forecast level of £900 in the government's Interim National Development Plan of July 1987. With the commissioning of the third tailings plant, ZCCM was forecasting activity at 470,000-to 490,000-ton levels in 1987, well above those suggested in the World Bank's 1986 Economic Memorandum. But the fixing of the exchange rate at ZK8 to the dollar in May 1987 is likely to squeeze ZCCM severely beginning in 1988 as positive earnings are highly dependent upon a favourable exchange rate. Together with the increased uncertainty now regarding G-7 growth prospects in 1988, one ought to be less sanguine concerning copper prices in the near future and futures markets are reflecting that trend.

In summary, the economic reform program did help to arrest the rate of decline of the Zambian economy but not sufficiently so as to build adequate political or public support for the reforms being undertaken. The economy performed poorly for a number of reasons, some of which were external to the ERP itself. The dollar value of exports stagnated in the short term as world copper prices continued to be weak and even as some cost reductions and productivity improvements by ZCCM were achieved. The devaluation did, however, assist the mining industry's cash flow and so permit the mining industry to provide revenue to the government.

A principal factor undermining the recovery though was the rising burden of servicing Zambia's foreign debt (see the Appendix to Chapter 1 for a detailed analysis). The continued, and extreme, scarcity of foreign exchange for intermediate inputs, spare parts and raw materials caused significant bottlenecks and, thus, supply constraints to renewing growth. With import shortages affecting all sectors – productive and consumption – it is not surprising that in the short run, import demand did not fall as a result of devaluation.

Devaluation and diversification

A key element in the structural adjustment program was to imple- ment an effective real devaluation of the Zambian kwacha. This was done on the basis of a foreign exchange auction process which began in October 1985. Auctioning of foreign exchange is a recent and highly experimental attempt at implementing and maintaining devaluation in the Third World (see Quirk, 1987, pp. 32-35). Few African economies have been prepared to allocate scarce foreign exchange through such a system fearing that such a thin market might well lead to disruptive speculation by traders, and/or to a significant increase in non-essential imports at the expense of higher priority import needs for investment goods. Under pressure from the Fund and the World Bank to devalue, the Zambian government accepted to implement an auction system, although dissenting voices inside government continued to warn against such a policy.

This section offers a summary of the main features of the Zambian auction system and its major impact. A growing literature on the Zambian experience is now appearing and has informed this analysis; this is also reflected in the bibliography (see in particular, Quirk, Jalakis and Economics Association of Zambia, all 1987).

Devaluation did alter the distribution of imports to different sectors of the economy but the principal and most direct effect of the devaluation was to increase kwacha import prices. A small number of firms in the manufacturing and trading sectors were able to take advantage of the foreign exchange available in the auction although, unexpectedly, agriculture took relatively little.

These price increases were passed on to manufacturers and then to consumers and contributed to inflationary pressures more generally in the economy. The devaluation did not lead in the short run to efficient import substitution in the Zambian case, given the structural rigidities in the economy.

With respect to exports, given the volume and quality of Zambia's mineral deposits and the state of longer term world demand for copper, it is unwise to base sustained export growth for Zambia on copper alone. However, in the short period in which the reform program operated, there was insufficient time to allow non-traditional exporters to fully exploit available opportunities. Finally, the exchange rate became destabilized about one year after the auction had begun and, together with the impact on prices, this uncertainty contributed to the government's decision to abandon the Fund/Bank structural adjustment effort.

Devaluation had two objectives:

- to encourage export diversification away from the mining industry and to enhance the overall level of export earnings; and
- to encourage efficient import substitution and to rationalize the allocation of scarce foreign exchange through the market mechanism of supply and demand.

There was a weekly auction of foreign exchange beginning in October,1985. Initially, oil, ZCCM, IATA and fertilizer imports were exempted from the auction, although their payments were made at the prevailing rate. The supply of foreign exchange was exhausted by the marginal bid and that became the prevailing rate until the following auction. Import licences were still required but were issued against 5 percent of the value of imported goods. The Bank of Zambia retained the right to refuse any application for foreign exchange without reason. 'No funds involved' licences – for those with retained foreign exchange – were issued free, but a 5 percent tax was imposed in August 1986.

The Zambian kwacha fell by 55 percent in the opening auction to ZK5.01 to the dollar and US$5 million was allocated to the auction. By February 1986, the auction was increased to $9 million but oil, ZCCM and fertilizers now bid inside the auction system. Initial experience with the auction seemed quite positive as a devaluation of about 68 percent relative to the U.S. dollar had brought the official rate much closer to the parallel rate. Then a series of events served to undermine private and public confidence in the auction system.

By mid-1986, some administrative amendments aimed at stabilizing the rate and improving revenue collection on import taxes, and the introduction of a 'Dutch' auction system, where bid price is equal to the buy price, contributed to uncertainty in the market and the rate moved above ZK8 to the U.S. dollar and then fell to ZK8. The government was trying to contain speculative bidding against the kwacha by introducing the Dutch auction procedure.

The government had made significant and highly visible changes to the economic management team which fuelled speculation that it was about to abandon the auction system. When the kwacha rate began to fall relative to the dollar, in July 1986, there was a demand for US$22 million in the auction of mid-July 1986. It was becoming evident that the government's attempts to strengthen the kwacha were failing. The government had become concerned with the strong reaction by organized labour to the inflationary impact of the devaluation. By intervening, it had hoped to weigh against expectations of further depreciation in the rate. Its actions, however, created a strong and opposite reaction in the market which resulted in further pressure on the rate. When the government was unable to meet the demand for foreign exchange from mid-July, a growing pipeline built up and disbursements slowed, adding further downward pressure from the auction on the rate.

In October 1986, the supply of foreign exchange was reduced to US$5.5 million and the rate rose to ZK13.48 to the dollar, a devaluation of 83 percent relative to the pre-auction rate. Bidders were sensing that the government had lost confidence in the auction system. When maize prices were decontrolled in December 1986 and consumption subsidies dropped abruptly, the rate had reached ZK14.92. In January 1987, the president ended the auction and introduced a dual rate with one window for government purchases and a second window for all other purposes. The rate at the second window hit ZK22 by the beginning of May 1987. The government announced that the rate would be set at ZK8 to the dollar and that debt service would be limited to 10 percent of export earnings, net of strategic payments. The government stated this would amount to US$30 million in debt servicing against scheduled payments of US$500-600 million.

A preliminary assessment
of the auction system

The auction system did achieve the principal objective of an effective real devaluation of the kwacha. It did so, however, by means of a sharp shock, especially after mid-1986, rather than a more measured and politically acceptable devaluation. Given the relative thinness of the market in Zambia for foreign exchange, speculative destabilization was a reality which the government had to try to offset as best it could with the limited foreign exchange at its disposal.

The objective of the structural adjustment program should have been the implementation of a more orderly devaluation of the kwacha. If an auctioning system was necessary to achieve such an objective, a greater supply of foreign exchange from external sources was needed, and given Zambia's macroeconomic distress, it could afford this only on concessional terms.

A real, effective devaluation could have been accomplished by a variety of different policy instruments and it is by no means clear that, prima facie, an auctioning mechanism is superior. Recent analysis of flexible and market-determined rates of exchange for developing countries suggests that destabilizing speculation can be an important factor and that successful devaluation does require that economic agents see tangible progress in the decline of inflation (Quirk et al, 1987, p. 34). In Zambia the latter requirement never materialized.

The auction 'failed' for a number of complex and interrelated reasons. The government's own commitment to the auction varied over time and this contributed to undermining confidence in the auction. There were the additional administrative regulations, the changes in the economic management team, the government's desire to stabilize the rate and its inability to supply US$22 million in response to bids at one point which could have served to dampen demand and speculation.

Underfinancing for the auction, by itself, did not cause the government to abandon the auction, although given the persistent scarcity of foreign exchange, it must have had an important contributory influence. In the main, however, donor agencies and financial institutions did live up to their commitments to the auction system although there are reports of delays in funding which disrupted the smooth functioning of the auction.

The principal reasons for the abandonment of the auction were the growing instability in the rate by mid-1986, to which the government's interventions had contributed, and the rising inflation rate, itself a reflection in part of the devaluation.

More generally, the government's inability to contain the growth in the stock of the money supply, which reflected the fiscal deficit, (and itself driven by the debt-servicing burden) harmed the ERP and contributed to the collapse of the Fund/Bank structural adjustment effort. If the government had been able to control the growth in the fiscal deficit and the money supply, it is possible that the exchange rate could have been stabilized at a real rate consistent with profitability in the mining sector and which would have allowed for some export diversification over time. Whether the stabilized real rate would have permitted more efficient import allocation through price rationing or led to price increases because of the high inelasticity of demand for imports by the productive sectors, both manufacturing and agriculture, is difficult to determine and the answer still speculative. However, on the basis of preliminary and qualitative assessments, there is reason to believe that a kwacha dollar rate around ZK12 would, if maintained in real terms (that is, steadily adjusted downwards in nominal terms), meet the objectives of export competitiveness and potential diversification while encouraging efficient import substitution.

The government is currently open to consultation on mechanisms to achieve these objectives but is not prepared to accept a return to the auction system. Therefore, there may emerge a foreign exchange policy in which the kwacha will not appreciate in real terms against say a trade-weighted basket of currencies. This could involve consideration of a range of alternatives including a managed 'crawl' downwards, a peg to the SDR or one cross rate, or a basket of currencies. Given the importance of this issue for macroeconomic policy, it is one of the areas noted for further work in the final chapter.

The strengths of a liberalized system are that it should guard against 'bureaucratic' determination of the exchange rate and serve to allocate a very scarce resource in a more timely manner according to priority uses. Those strengths should not be undervalued in whatever replacement mechanism is adopted.

Given the rigidities in the Zambian economy and the scarcity of policy managers, the auction system, in the context of the more wide ranging policy reforms under way, suffered from 'too much change too quickly'. Liberalization created too many demands for change in the Zambian economy. Together with the lack of a more positive set of external economic conditions which could have contributed to more robust growth, these set the scene for public and political dissatisfaction with the auction system. The exchange rate is often a barometer for politicians and the public of a nation's well-being and the signals in early 1987 were read as placing Zambia on the critical list once again.

With an already high debt-servicing burden, devaluation put additional short-term pressure on the fiscal system to meet its external obligations. The kwacha costs of debt servicing rose and, in an already inflationary environment where government was under strong pressure to reduce its own consumption and thus unable to contribute to any improvement in private consumption levels, domestic support for the program eroded and the devaluation through the auction system was an immediate and visible target.

Public finance and inflation

The Economic Recovery Program aimed at reducing government's influence on the rate of inflation by reducing the public sector deficit through expenditure restraint and revenue enhancement measures.

Each of these objectives was partially achieved in the initial stages of the reform program but was then undone under the interrelated pressures of declining real per capita consumption levels, price increases induced by the kwacha devaluation, and the government's inability to control the fiscal deficit. By 1986, the deficit had begun to widen again under the combined impact of the kwacha devaluation and rising debt charges. Revenues initially were buoyant as higher import duties and a new mineral export tax contributed to higher public sector income (see Table 9). But the revenue sources were not sufficiently elastic to decrease the deficit on a sustained basis.

As the government financed the growing fiscal deficit, through recourse to the domestic banking system primarily, it contributed to higher inflation and more pronounced falls in real consumption levels. At the end of 1986, the fiscal deficit had become a major source of inflationary pressure in the economy, having risen nearly fourfold from 1985 (see Table 9).

The 'straw which was to break the camel's back' was the removal of the maize subsidy at the end of 1986. The government had announced the initial policy intention – to remove the subsidy – in September 1986 at the time that it had renewed negotiations with the IMF to restore flows to the auction. As a part of that negotiation, Zambia agreed to a broader set of reforms including the removal of maize consumption subsidies. With hindsight it is clear that the subsidy removal was very badly handled, both technically and more importantly, politically, by the government.

In November 1986, the government announced that consumer prices were to increase to ZK55 per 90 kg bag, up from the ZK35 per bag paid at the time to NAMBOARD and the co-ops. This represented a 57 percent increase in retail prices. The initial policy announcements were quite unequivocal that roller meal, a staple of the lower-income groups, would not be affected by the new measures immediately, however, roller maze was unavailable. When the policy was implemented in December 1986, the actual retail prices were ZK77 per bag, a full 25 percent above the 57 percent increase which had been anticipated when the policy was first announced only three months previously.

The resultant extreme scarcity of roller meal (the government blamed the millers for substituting breakfast meal for roller meal in order to maximize their returns, while the millers blamed retailers for hoarding stocks of roller meal to widen retail margins) led to a widening display of disaffection. Led by the poorest consumers, rioting erupted in major urban centres, resulting in 15 deaths. The government had to declare an emergency situation. Already faced with significant and sustained losses in their real consumption levels, they could no longer face the prospect of further erosion.

After economic reform

The government could no longer sustain a reform program which did not provide evidence of recovery. The subsidy was restored; the millers were nationalized; and by mid-1987, the government had abandoned the Economic Reform Program and announced its intention to embark upon a 'New Economic Recovery Program' through an Interim National Development Plan (GRZ, 1987a).

The basic objectives of the new program appear to be sound enough. In the context of a rapid decline in real per person consumption and income, the government is seeking to increase the rate of economic growth, (in part by directly limiting the payment of external obligations); to reduce inflationary pressures (by repegging the kwacha/dollar exchange rate); and, to target scarce foreign exchange to the highest priority needs as well as to target subsidy payments to those most in need.

The ERP had not achieved sufficient progress on any of these counts. Growth was inadequate to provide per capita increases; devaluation had contributed, in the context of huge external obligations, to a large increase in the fiscal deficit and inflationary pressures. With Zambia's exhibited dependence on copper and the structural weaknesses of the economy to adjust away from that dependence, in the short run the ERP was bound to fail. It placed major demands for adjustment on the economy as debt payments rose and copper exports were stagnant; it put inordinate 'fast-track' pressure on the government to remove subsidies even as consumption was declining and to implement other sweeping changes in an abrupt period.

While the government of Zambia had good reasons to abandon the ERP, there are several questions which must be raised concerning the assumptions and mechanisms contained in the new Interim National Development Plan, announced in detail in July, 1987.

The estimated increase in GDP bears inadequate relationship to the foreign exchange constraints which are a constant factor in the Zambian situation. A forecast growth rate of 2.2 percent seems optimistic in the circumstances, and some of the sectoral growth rates, such as 4.8 percent for manufacturing, given its import dependence, look particularly unrealistic. GDP expenditure figures suggest that private consumption will grow faster than total GDP during the plan period – by 3.6 percent – and that real investment will be a very buoyant 46 percent higher at the end of 1988 than currently. These increases are to be financed by a drop in government consumption as foreign debt-servicing payments fall, but are principally driven by a 17 percent increase in real exports. Despite current strength in world copper prices, these projections appear optimistic in light of the current exchange rate regime and its impact on ZCCM's profitability and on non-traditional exports.

But the projected budget figures are the most suspect. Government subsidies will rise from 12 percent of recurrent expenditure to 23 percent between 1986 and 1988, while debt payments will fall from 33 percent to 2.6 percent over the same period. The large increase in gross fixed capital formation assumed in the interim plan does not tally with the government's own capital expenditures which are frozen over the plan period. Real recurrent expenditure falls as well and there is no provision for increasing civil service wages which is unrealistic in the current circumstances of falling consumption levels.

The reimposition of comprehensive price controls has led to increased efforts to avoid formal regulations. Recent newspaper accounts suggest that enforcement will be a major problem for the government and that shortages are already beginning to emerge for basic consumer goods.

In order for the INDP to achieve its objectives, there is a need to review the exchange rate regime, the fiscal program including both expenditures and revenues, and improved means to increase consumption without creating major new inflationary pressures. This latter objective could mean fewer price controls targeted to more basic consumption goods.

In summary, then, the Economic Reform Program of 1983-87 did help to arrest the rate of decline in real per capita consumption but was insufficient in restoring higher real levels. It did, however, have to face the reality of a rising debt burden, weak copper exports, severe import shortages and a lack of time in which the efficiency gains of the reform could have begun to offset the social costs and structural rigidities of the Zambian economy. The assumptions of the ERP were deficient in some respects as well; given the import dependency of the economy, the devaluation of the kwacha had to be inflationary. Import prices are expected to rise under a devaluation but import volumes, with a lag, should also decline as efficient import substitution occurs. The structural rigidities in Zambia will not lead to a price rationing of imports in the short term but an inflationary push as imports have failed to satisfy demand in the past. More time and more financing for imports were clearly needed in order for the ERP to have succeeded. There were, to be sure, weaknesses on the government's side too: the intervention in the auction was poorly conceived, and the removal of maize subsidies severely damaged the government's credibility, domestically and internationally.

5

Implications
for
donors

This chapter, though not a comprehensive assessment of donor programs in Zambia, is intended to serve the more limited purpose of identifying key issues for that community to consider in programming assistance to Zambia.

Exchange rate policy

In the main, donor response to the economic recovery program was one of positive optimism that the structural adjustment effort was long overdue and that, therefore, the basic objectives of the ERP were to be encouraged and supported. This was particularly true of the exchange rate policy and movement to a foreign exchange auction in 1985-86. Most donors, both the international financial institutions and bilateral aid agencies, were immediate and full supporters of the exchange auction system. Together they financed about one-half of the foreign exchange passing through the auction system. As noted in the earlier discussion of the auction system it 'failed' due to a variety of factors, some of which were clearly beyond the control of the Zambian government. If the political commitment to a greater degree of flexibility in the exchange rate materializes in the future, it should be an important priority of donors to assist the government, if asked, to establish policies and operational mechanisms to manage the exchange rate system in a way that meets the goals of an ordered devaluation and an effective and efficient allocation of this particularly scarce commodity.

Debt relief

It is patently clear that there will be no growth in the Zambian context without further debt relief. This remains an immediate need and one to which careful attention and some creative solutions are required.

Zambia's scheduled debt servicing had for some time become unsustainable. The 10 percent limitation unilaterally invoked by the government in 1987 was a recognition of this and creates a de facto debt relief for Zambia. However, it is a unilateral initiative and, while it may well increase net financial transfers in the short term, it does leave the issue of longer-term flows very much an open question.

There is an urgent need for greater cooperation between Zambia and the international financial community with respect to new external capital flows and the treatment of past loans. The problem has two main components.

a) Existing non-concessional bilateral loans to Zambia must be reduced through write-offs, write-downs, interest rate reductions or more generous rescheduling. But this will depend on the political will of the individual creditors. A significant proportion of this debt is held by official, or near official, creditors as import financing and has been rescheduled under past Paris Club arrangements. There will be a need to consider further relief on interest charges associated with Paris Club arrangements for Zambia and other low-income, debt-distressed countries. But the evidence from the most recent effort at structural adjustment is unequivocal: Zambia cannot sustain debt servicing at recent historical levels and achieve adjustment with growth.

b) Multilateral debt, carrying preferred creditor status, has grown to become a substantial proportion of total debt. Fund credits in particular have grown quickly and repayment is due in the short run unless even additional arrears are to be accumulated. The government's decision to limit debt payments has meant the accumulation of further Fund arrears and the inability of the government to access Fund facilities. Bilateral donors are now faced with delicate policy decisions on whether or not to continue balance of payments assistance to Zambia as it falls further into arrears to its preferred creditors.

Canada's decisions, first, to move to an all grant aid program beginning in fiscal year 1986/87, and in May 1986 to provide a renewable five-year debt moratorium to selected African countries undergoing policy reforms (and later to convert this to debt relief for official development assistance for many countries) is a model for other bilateral donors to consider. While Canada's record in this regard is admirable, it is only a modest contribution to the overall debt burden for Zambia, and Export Development Corporation (EDC) and Canadian Wheat Board debt remains untouched.

Program aid

With Zambia's structural dependence on imports for short-run economic growth, donor efforts to provide import support are particularly needed. Ideally this would involve program aid offering free foreign exchange. If this is not acceptable to donors, a second best, short-term response would be to match Zambia's import requirements to donor supply availabilities (tied aid in effect). Recent indications that Japan and the European Community are to provide liquid program assistance is encouraging and should help Zambia avoid a further reduction in imports.

Interim national development plan (INDP)

Many donors express concern about the assumptions and policy mechanisms to achieve the main objectives contained in the INDP, but there is an agreed sense that the basic objectives of the plan are sound and could therefore be supported. The INDP has several shortcomings which need to be discussed with the government including the current exchange rate policy, the need to reform the budget, to review the mechanisms employed for protecting consumers by price controls and the impact of stagnation on the poorest.

There is scope for donors to look very carefully at their individual programs and projects to ensure that they meet the criteria of contributing in a direct way to economic growth and/or increasing the consumption of the poorest in Zambia.

Individual projects need to be reviewed to ensure that they are achieving a positive real rate of return to invested funds and that aid program objectives are consistent with the criteria mentioned above.

6

Issues for
further
research

In this final chapter of Part I, there is an initial list of further research issues following the review of Zambia's experience with economic policy reform and attempted, but unfulfilled, adjustment.

Foreign exchange policy

Because Zambia has abandoned the foreign exchange auction, one should not necessarily interpret this to mean that all avenues to changes in the policies governing foreign exchange have been closed. There is, if not a consensus, a widely held belief within Zambia that the kwacha/dollar rate should be allowed to change over time in an orderly way in order to promote the structural adjustments in the Zambian economy which are so necessary. What is at issue is the precise mechanism which would allow the objectives of export diversification and a more market-oriented allocation of foreign exchange to be pursued. This would have to include controls against speculative disruption which induces uncertainty for both the private and public sector, and a requirement that priority uses would be met first.

Some flexibility in the nominal exchange rate is necessary as is a measure of stability in the real rate. It could be quite relevant to Zambian policy makers to discuss research which would identify these potential alternatives and their likely consequences. Given the government's experience with the auction system, there should be scope for work that would encompass the set of relevant policy and technical issues here.

The options could include, without limiting other possibilities, a dual exchange rate system with a more stable real, but adjustable, nominal rate for debt payments and essential imports such as oil, fertilizer, industrial sector inputs and possibly ZCCM exports. A second window could exist for all other foreign exchange transactions and could be a floating rate. This could cover consumer goods and other transactions such as remittances.

Macroeconomic policy management

One of the key aspects of the ERP was the difficulty the Zambian government encountered in controlling the macroeconomic policy environment. The government faced enormous challenges of coping with the negative impact of external shocks and debt servicing which made growth impossible while trying to maintain political support for the program.

Given the size of the 'structural deficit' in Zambia , it is critical that additional impetus be given to effective means to reduce that deficit without undermining the government's ability to assist those most in need. While debt relief is a part of this, with or without it, there is a need for a study of various means to enhance the elasticity of the tax system through possibly higher, or more comprehensive, import taxes which would improve the public sector's ability to collect taxes from those best able to pay.

Social impact of economic reform

Even as the World Bank is undertaking a series of studies to assess the impact and incidence of the maize subsidy, and reviewing public expenditures generally and specifically on health and public works, there may well be scope for additional research. This is not to prejudge the Bank's efforts in any way but to serve as a signal to the donor community that it may be worthwhile reviewing that work, once available, to ascertain if any gaps exist or if those studies suggest any additional research.

For example, it may be helpful for the government to look quite specifically at how to implement consumption subsidies for maize that would protect against the worst errors and abuses of December 1986. This could include the impact of targeting subsidies on the very poorest at the point of consumption through 'fair price' shops or some other variant. The fiscal, logistical and equity implications would be highly relevant to the government, donors and the poor in Zambia.

A current issue of some controversy involves the government's efforts at price controls. Recently, CIDA withdrew its support of the Prices and Incomes Commission because of its role in price control implementation. With the fall in real consumption – precise incidence cannot be gauged accurately – there may be sound reasons for controlling the prices of a more limited number of essential commodities to limit the adverse impact of price increases on the poor. At the same time, it would be necessary to investigate supply enhancing policies to help protect against shortages and parallel markets emerging for the controlled goods.

Export diversification

One of the shared goals of the government and its supporters is to diversify away from the current over-reliance upon copper and its derivatives for foreign exchange earnings. The prospects for exploiting Zambia's comparative advantages in agriculture and manufacturing are intimately tied to the exchange rate. Most observers agree that at a rate of ZK8 to the dollar, non-traditional exports will suffer. The Interim National Development Plan gives strong endorsement to the objective of diversification although there are no specific implementing policies to achieve this objective.

Related then to research on exchange rate policies would be research to identify the specific elements of macroeconomic policy most likely to influence exporters of new products (for example, tariff and tax policies, infrastructure facilities, etc.) which could help identify the most important constraints and thus the most effective policy initiatives.

Agriculture policy implementation

As chronicled in several reports, Zambia has not met its potential in terms of agricultural production. Recent suggestions for reform have included raising producer prices, initiating more market-oriented commodity procurement and transportation policies and less reliance on the state for distribution and pricing of inputs.

It may be an opportune moment to review these issues in light of Zambia's experience with the ERP. CIDA is playing a major role in production technology and technical assistance in the sector and it could be highly relevant to look at a wide range of policy, technical and development assistance issues at a sectoral level.

Part II

Living without the IMF

7

The "Growth from Our Own Resources" effort

Introduction

The failure of the IMF-sponsored Economic Recovery Program (ERP) owed much to design faults and to severe structural problems in the Zambian economy, namely Zambia's extreme dependence on copper and its unmanageable burden of external debt. Added to this was a chequered record of policy implementation. The combination of these factors led to a break in relations with the IMF in May 1987 and an announcement by President Kaunda that Zambia would follow a path of 'Growth From Our Own Resources'.

In July 1987, the Government of Zambia announced a new economic recovery program in the form of an Interim National Development Plan (INDP) which would be operative until December 1988. This was followed in December 1987 by a more substantial document which laid our more fully Zambia's objections to the IMF structural adjustment package and which provided more detailed sectoral and regional components of the INDP. In January 1989, the Fourth National Development Plan was introduced, running from 1989 through 1992.

What is important about these initiatives is that they were designed without IMF/World Bank policy input and they do not depend upon capital flows from the international institutions. Given the dominance of the IMF/World Bank in shaping economic policy in sub-Saharan Africa today, it is crucially important that Zambia's go-it-alone policy be examined carefully, not merely as a possible remedy for Zambia's own economic difficulties, but also as a possible model to be followed by other countries in Africa.

The analysis begins with an assessment of the basic objectives of the INDP which remain the key objectives for the whole period of the Fourth Plan. It then examines the underlying strategies, assesses economic performance, evaluates the strengths and weaknesses of the made-in-Zambia approach and, finally, suggests ways in which the approach might be improved.

Objectives of the interim national development plan

The objectives of the Plan were specified as follows:

- to release resources for development by compressing non-essential and luxury imports and limiting debt-service payments;
- to reactivate the economy by increasing capacity utilization in enterprises producing essential or basic goods or goods for export;
- to stabilize the economy by controlling inflation;
- to promote a self-sustaining economy through increased profitability and reinvestment of profits in enterprises utilizing local raw materials;
- to diversify exports by promoting non-traditional exports and exports of manufactured goods;
- to restructure production and consumption patterns so as to use foreign exchange as a strategic resource;
- to increase employment opportunities through the establishment of village and small-scale industries based on local raw materials;
- to increase the government's capacity to manage the economy; and
- to reduce subsidies gradually and target them to the needy (GoZ,1987 p5).

Strategies of the plan

The strategies adopted were a reaffirmation and extension of the measures announced by President Kaunda in May 1987. The exchange rate was to remain administered and 'stabilized'. For most of the Interim Plan period it remained at eight kwacha (K8) to the US$, while in November 1988 a 25 percent devaluation took it to K10. The allocation of foreign exchange was also to be achieved through administrative means, a Foreign Exchange Management Committee (FEMAC) being established for this purpose. The guidelines for this committee were to reduce luxury imports and concentrate on essential consumer goods, raw materials, services and capital goods. To this end, and representing a sharp break with past policy, the plan restricted servicing of foreign debt to no more than 10 percent of net export earnings i.e., export earnings after deducting the foreign-exchange requirements of the copper industry (ZCCM), oil imports, Zambia Airways (IATA) and fertilizer imports. These deductions meant, effectively, that no more than an estimated 6.5 percent of export earnings would be devoted to debt-servicing, while the nominal debt servicing burden of the country at that time was in the region of 100 percent of exports, or 150 percent if arrears are taken into account (Young,1988).

As an anti-inflationary device, interest rates were controlled, at between 15 to 20 percent per year until November 1988 when the upper limit was raised to 25 percent, as were the prices of a wide range of consumer goods. Initially, there were no fewer than 21 goods on the price control list, but it was anticipated that by January 1989, the number would be reduced to a dozen. The items still controlled are expected to be maize meal, milk, beer, cooking oil, school uniforms, candles, kerosene, soap/detergent, sugar, salt, baby food and shoes.

By the judicious allocation of scarce resources, the Plan aimed to raise the level of capacity utilization in local industry and build a profit base for reinvestment. The emphasis was to be on strengthening local linkages through the more extensive use of local raw materials, and on adopting more labour-intensive techniques of production in order to create more jobs. Non-traditional exports were to be encouraged but these industries, it was argued, would need to adopt 'modern and competitive technologies'.

While not laying out a comprehensive strategy for regulating or shaping income distribution, the plan document argued that an incomes policy was required both to ensure the stimulation of effective demand and to ensure the retention and recruitment of skilled and efficient staff in the civil service. Under the first heading, it was felt that purchasing power had fallen in the economy and so in order to raise capacity utilization, a minimum wage had to be established, and wages had to be allowed to rise 'through collective bargaining, and through income support programs for the unemployed'. Under the latter, the government pledged to pursue a policy of making the salaries and conditions of service in the civil service competitive with those of other sectors.

Improving and consolidating the civil service was seen to be integral to improving the capacity of the state to play a leading role in both the activities, and the management, of the mixed economy. The Plan asserted the need for strengthening both decentralization and participatory democracy, as well as for redefining the role of the state in the economy.

It is apparent, therefore, that there are major differences in policy approach from the orthodox adjustment programs of the IMF/World Bank. The emphasis on fairly fixed prices, exchange rates and interest rates, the state allocation of foreign exchange, the reaffirmation of the important role of the state in industrial policy and, finally, a very strong emphasis on income distribution – all constitute significant departures from adjustment orthodoxy.

Performance under the plan

What follows evaluates economic performance of the Zambian economy during the brief duration of the INDP. It does so by examining the main performance criteria viz, GDP growth, balance-of-payments performance, fiscal and monetary performance and the movement of prices.

Gross domestic product

In terms of real GDP growth, the last two years have been moderately successful. The Interim Plan projected a growth rate of 2.2 percent per year, which was achieved in 1987 and surpassed (2.7 percent) in 1988. Robust growth in the manufacturing sector was enjoyed in both years (see Table 11), with projections being exceeded and the mining and service sectors performed well in 1987. In 1988, the recovery of agricultural production was the principal factor explaining overall growth performance, and was greatly in excess of expectations. This was the first time since 1979-81 that Zambia had experienced two consecutive years of economic growth.

This growth record must, however, be put into proper perspective. Since population growth remains very high, at between 3.4 and 3.6 percent per year, per capita incomes in Zambia continued to fall over the Interim Plan period as they have done in every year since 1981. This fact emphasizes the utter inadequacy of plan targets for overall growth in GDP.

A word of caution is in order in using GDP figures. GDP estimates are very crude and subject to quite large adjustments. Thus in the Progress Report on the Plan issued in June 1988, GDP growth for 1987 was estimated to have been negative, at -0.2 percent. Subsequent upward adjustments were made to estimates for the mining, manufacturing and trade sectors. Secondly, the Plan estimates were also very crude and covered 18 months instead of the usual 12, which means that they were unduly conservative in terms of annual growth rates. Thirdly, as will be argued later, it appears that black market and unofficial transactions generally have increased significantly over the past year, and these are not recorded in the official statistics.

The almost unrelieved tendency for per capita incomes to fall over the last decade has led to a decline in the savings rate, as people have attempted to maintain consumption standards. While the Interim Plan sought to reverse this trend by sharply reducing the proportion of consumption in real income, and by greatly increasing the rate of investment, Table 11 shows that these efforts were only partially successful. While the consumption rate did fall, it fell by much less than planned, and was not accompanied by an increase in the investment rate: indeed, the investment rate continued to fall. This is most likely explained by the loss of project aid following the break with the Fund/Bank, and the continuing tautness of the foreign exchange constraint. Since the current account balance of payments appears to have improved over this period, it seems that the improved domestic savings rate was offset by a larger budget deficit.

In terms of explaining the growth performance of different sectors of the economy, it is to be noted that agricultural growth patterns over the past two years have been mainly weather determined. 1987 was a drought year while 1988 was a year of very favourable weather. As a result, total maize production fell by 13.6 percent in 1987 to 11.8 million bags, and rose by 36.6 percent in 1988 to 16.1 million bags, while marketed maize output fell by 31 percent in 1987 to 7.3 million bags, and rose by 55 percent in 1988 to 11.3 million bags. The gap between production and marketing reflects producers holding back maize for their own consumption and, possibly, blockages in the state agricultural marketing system.

The improved performance of the manufacturing sector is explained by the policy of according this sector a high priority in the foreign exchange allocation system. During the first nine months of FEMAC, it received $165 million in allocations compared with only $110 during 17 months of the auction. (INDP, Progress Report No. 2 1988, p. 22.) The record of the crucially important mining sector is more difficult to explain. World copper prices were at record height, but unfortunately, the industry was unable to capitalize on these prices in 1988, when copper output actually fell by 5 percent and, as we shall see, copper exports were well below planned levels. The reason for this was a shortfall in output due not to ore production per se, but to shortages of locally produced sulphuric acid and problems with aging smelters. While shortages of foreign exchange played a role here, they did so not directly through ZCCM which claims it is happy with its annual allocation, but rather through local suppliers of goods and services to ZCCM. In particular, servicing of the great diversity of mining and smelting equipment, some of which is now aging, is becoming increasingly problematical.

Balance of payments

While realized world prices for copper were 20 percent higher than anticipated in 1987 and fully 52.4 percent better than forecast in 1988, the amount of copper exported fell by 12 percent relative to 1987 and by 11 percent relative to the planned target. It is regrettable that Zambia was not able to meet its export target for copper volume, as this would have increased foreign exchange earnings by some $122 million, permitting an increase in imports of about 16 percent over actual levels in 1988. What makes the situation even worse is that ZCCM was given a lump sum foreign exchange allocation of $300 million based on targeted output levels, but there is no evidence that this allocation was reduced in the light of the output shortfall. If it was not, then the foreign exchange allocation procedures need review. It made little sense in the past when the demand for foreign exchange by ZCCM seemed to be invariant to the price of foreign exchange; it makes even less sense if this demand is invariant also to output levels.

In spite of not meeting planned output targets for copper, export earnings did rise in 1988, by an impressive 19 percent, as a result of the favourable world market conditions. This permitted an increase in imports of some 7 percent, or perhaps 3 percent in real terms, and a reduction in the current account balance-of-payments deficit by almost half.

It could be argued, therefore, that the improvement in the balance of payments owed little to domestic policy initiatives and much to the vagaries of the world market. This conclusion is reinforced by the disappointing performance of non-traditional exports in 1988. These remained stagnant at about $80 million, falling as a proportion of total exports from about 8 percent to about 7.7 percent. Since the nominal effective exchange rate appreciated by 57 percent between December

1986 and September 1988, and the *real* effective exchange rate by as much as 280 percent! (see Table 12), it is remarkable that these earnings have not fallen in the face of severely reduced competitiveness. The explanation for this appears to be that exporters value the access to scarce foreign exchange which the government's 50 percent retention scheme affords, for this enables them to earn rents on production for local markets or on sales of foreign exchange to third parties at market rates. Also, some exporters may have benefited from the direct allocation of foreign exchange by FEMAC.

In recognition of the growing misalignment of the exchange rate, the Government devalued the Kwacha by 25 percent in $ terms in November 1988. It also delinked the Kwacha from the US dollar and tied it to the SDR.

Assessing the impact of Zambia's *debt servicing* strategy is not an easy matter since reliable data is hard to come by, but the following estimates are at least indicative of recent developments in this area. At the end of 1987, the level of arrears on external payments had reached $1.3 billion, of which arrears to the IMF amounted to about $460 million, and the World Bank $87 million (at end of April 1988). For 1988, arrears will rise by the difference between servicing obligations and 10 percent of net exports. Net exports are likely to have reached about $750 million, since total exports were $1,165 million, and oil imports were about $84 million, fertilizers about $13 million, IATA payments about $19 million and ZCCM allocations (including debt servicing) about $300 million.

As far as one can tell, foreign interest charges (including those of the IMF) amounted to about $328 million while amortization payments (inclusive of $192 million IMF repurchases but *excluding* ZCCM obligations of an estimated $120 million) should have reached $386 million. Thus, according to Zambia's debt-servicing formula, only $75 million would have been paid out of a total obligation of $714 million. This reduces to 6.4 percent of total exports or to 10.5 percent of non-ZCCM obligations. More accurately, however, one ought to include the servicing of ZCCM debt, and if one does, then debt servicing payments were the equivalent of 16.7 percent of total exports and 23 percent of total obligations. The net result was that arrears on debt servicing payments rose by about $640 million last year, bringing total arrears to at least $1.9 billion in 1988. Thus the debt continues to grow despite the fact that there is no access to new loans.

Fiscal and monetary performance

Fiscal data are notoriously unreliable. There is no consistent data series available for this period, but Table 13 draws on the Interim Plan, budget estimates, the Fourth National Development Plan for estimated actual out-turn in 1987, and the 1988/89 budget address for actual out-turn in 1988. Difficulties of interpreting fiscal data are compounded further by having a third of the 1987 period (January-April) under the IMF program and the remaining two-thirds under the NERP. What the available data appear to show, however, is that the actual overall budget deficit in 1987, at K1.17 billion, was 43 percent less than originally budgeted and 21 percent less than the lower Interim Plan target. The principal reasons for this favourable outcome appear to be that expenditure on subsidies was a third less than anticipated by the plan, and interest payments were K300 million less than planned. Government borrowing from the banking system, at K1.18 billion was, however, K160 million higher than envisaged by the Plan because net external funding was actually negative as opposed to the planned level of almost K400 million. This level of borrowing was unquestionably inflationary, as it was equal to 29 percent of the broad money stock at the end of 1986. Indeed, broad money supply grew by 54 percent in 1987 and government borrowing accounted for over a half of this expansion.

It must be noted that the above budgetary figures differ quite markedly in some respects from those to be found in the latest IMF Article IV Consultation Report on Zambia (1988). This arrives at an overall deficit for 1987 of K3.3 billion on a commitment basis, and K2.2 billion on a cash basis. These differences are probably explained by the different ways in which debt servicing obligations have been treated. The official Zambian figures used in Table 13 appear to include only servicing commitments actually met, whereas the IMF includes all commitments, whether met or not. When allowance is made for arrears, the net deficit to be financed from the domestic banking system is very close on both approaches, the IMF arriving at a slightly higher figure of K1.3 billion.

Turning to 1988, it is apparent that the budget led to a significant *upward* revision of the Interim Plan targets for both revenue and expenditure. The main explanation for this appears to have been a decision by the government to raise the salaries of civil servants by 50 percent, presumably in a bid to offset some of the erosion of purchasing power occasioned by high rates of inflation. Interest payments also rose by K0.5 billion relative to the Interim Plan figure, presumably as a result of more careful budgeting. These increases were to be financed by an unanticipated, windfall, payment of income tax by ZCCM of some K0.7 billion, presumably on account of the impact of higher kwacha earnings in 1987 as a result of the rapid depreciation of the Kwacha in the final months of the auction, and as a result of the higher world copper prices in that year. Increased revenues were also anticipated from sales tax on imports, from excise taxes, and from enhanced inflows of foreign capital grants. Nevertheless, the overall deficit was expected to rise by K1.5 billion to K2.7 billion. This would have implied an increase in the proportion of the deficit to GDP from 6.4 percent in 1987 to 15 percent in 1988. It is little wonder that the 1988 budget drew criticism from both within Zambia (Institute for African Studies, 1988) and from without (IMF, 1988) for its likely inflationary impact.

In the event, it appears that the actual out-turn in 1988 was much closer to budget than was the case in the previous year. The overall deficit, at K2.5 billion, was the equivalent of 13.8 percent of GDP, or of 40 percent of broad money supply at the end of 1987. It appears that money supply is likely to have grown by at least 50 percent last year. Once again, it is to be noted that the overall deficit on the IMF's calculations is much higher, reaching K4.5 billion on a commitment basis: this figure serves as a constant reminder that underlying the official budget figures lies an unresolved, and growing, problem of foreign debt.

It is worth noting that, in spite of the general inflation of fiscal magnitudes, in real terms the expenditure on personal emoluments in 1988 was only 60 percent of its 1985 level, while non-staff departmental expenditures were only 75 percent of their 1985 level. In real terms, therefore, the recurrent budget continues to be eroded in most areas except interest payments and subsidies.

Prices

The rate of inflation in Zambia has risen steadily since the introduction of the INDP, from a year-on rate of 39.9 percent in July 1987 to 59.2 percent in July 1988. There seems to be some moderation in this rate from July, but even the September rate is in excess of 50 percent per year, which makes official statements of much lower rates for the year as a whole, in the region of 30-35 percent per year (Budget Statement, November 1988 p.7) look grossly over optimistic. It is generally believed that the real rate is even higher than the September figures would indicate since throughout 1988 the wide range of commodities subject to price control were often available only at much higher black market prices, which are not captured in official statistics. This trend in the rate of inflation led the Minister of Finance to complain that merchants did not reduce prices when the Kwacha was revalued and, indeed raised prices in December 1988 by much more than the rate of devaluation in that month. He did recognize, however, that the budget deficit and shortages of goods were primarily responsible for the continuing high rates of inflation. Furthermore, the Minister acknowledged that smuggling and black marketeering had recently become major problems indicating the 'malfunctioning of the economy, particularly the price mechanism'(Ibid p.6).

It appears from Table 14 that the acute switch in exchange rate policy over the past two years has had a bigger negative impact on lower income groups than on higher income groups. In 1986 inflation rates were higher for higher income groups than for lower; now the reverse appears to be the case, at least as far as the *official* rate of inflation is concerned. The explanation for this is that the import content of consumption is lower for lower income groups than for higher ones, so that periods of sharp devaluation raise the cost of living more for higher income groups than for lower. Conversely, a revaluation restrains price increases for commodities not easily prone to black marketeering, such as fuel and power, and it is indeed the low rate of increase in prices of these items, and of rents which are often controlled for this group (together having a weight of one third of the price index) which explains the decline in the rate of price increase for the higher income group. It is to be emphasised that while maize meal prices have not increased since 1986, prices of other foodstuffs consumed by the low income group have risen dramatically. Thus, the 1988 prices of such staple items as sugar, chicken, dry beans and milk were all between 2.5 and 3 times their 1986 levels. These price developments must be borne in mind when assessing the distributional impact of the INDP.

Thus the typical indicators of direction of an economy provide some contradictory information. The gross domestic product actually grew at a more rapid rate during these two years, albeit unevenly through the sectors. However, expanded growth was still slower than the growth of population, thus meaning a per capita decline. The treasury was unable to fully benefit from increased copper prices because of dropping production. Nonetheless export earnings increased but so, paradoxically, did the debt. General fiscal and monetary performance in 1988 came close to the actual budget figures but proved inflationary with prices rising rapidly. An assessment of the success or failure of the Zambian experiment therefore requires a deeper exploration of these factors.

8

Evaluation
of
performance

It is apparent that the underlying economic situation in Zambia deteriorated in a number of important respects during the INDP, although this was masked to some degree by the quite favourable prices of copper on the world market. Perhaps the most serious indication of deterioration was the inability of ZCCM to raise copper export tonnage to take advantage of the high world prices. This reflects a great loss of opportunity to boost the economy by breaking through the import constraint. While prices are expected to remain high in the coming year, at US cents 125 compared with 117 for 1988, the forecast for 1990 is that prices will fall to around 90 cents per lb, so the boom will be quite short-lived. Clearly, the government has been delinquent in the allocation of foreign exchange, as it is unlikely that the returns to other sectors of the economy would have been greater than those to be had from ensuring the smooth functioning of industries crucial to copper production. It would have paid the government to switch foreign exchange to these industries or, though perhaps more difficult, borrow foreign exchange against assigned copper exports, even at high rates of interest, in order to be able to tap into the high world prices. Failure to realize full earnings potential in this, the dominant sector of the economy, must surely cast doubt on the efficacy of FEMAC as a mechanism of foreign exchange allocation.

The second indication of mounting economic problems and loss of control over the economy by the government, is the growth of the unofficial and black markets. By the end of 1988 these were very visible for a wide range of basic commodities, with long lineups in stores whenever new supplies arrived, many of the buyers acting simply as intermediaries channelling the goods elsewhere at higher prices. Likewise, smuggling to neighbouring countries is said to have increased substantially, especially of goods such as maize meal and fertilizer which are subject to domestic subsidization and price control. A less obvious but equally telling indication of policy weaknesses is the practice, sanctioned by government, of exporters transferring retained foreign exchange earnings to others at an exchange rate well in excess of the official one, say at three times the official rate (in contrast to the black market rate which runs at between five and eight times the official rate).

While it is, understandably, impossible to measure the scope of these unofficial market activities, their growth is corroborated to some extent by the increase in the importance of currency in the money supply. Thus, between 1986 and 1988, currency rose from 25.8 percent of M1 to 34.6 percent, at a time when M1 itself more than tripled in size. This is usually a clear indication of a radical shift in payments procedures, consistent with the rapid growth of unofficial market activities. Further evidence is available from frequent reports in local newspapers of police intercepting truck loads of goods, such as sugar being smuggled to Zaire (Times of Zambia, 1/12/88), or cassettes, cosmetics and similar goods being smuggled into the country from Swaziland or Mauritius (Ibid, 30/11/88). Close to 200 traders also had their licences revoked for allegedly black marketeering and smuggling (INDP, Second Progress Report, June 1988, p.158).

A third and related indicator is the failure of current policies to bring down the rate of inflation. This objective was one of the most important ones in the plan, as the main reason for abandoning the auction and revaluing the Kwacha was the unacceptable rate of price increases. It is to be noted, however, that efforts elsewhere in neighbouring countries, to bring down the rate of inflation by overvaluing the exchange rate, such as Tanzania between 1981 and 1984, or Uganda between 1986 and 1987, have failed equally miserably. The main reason is that the underlying supply situation for foreign exchange does not in any way improve by over-valuation and in fact usually deteriorates as exports shift to the black market. At the same time, the demand for exchange is inflated as a result of its relatively low price and, equally important, as a result of enhanced speculation about the likely future availability of exchange. In Zambia, the nature of the principal export, copper, is such that an overvalued Kwacha will not promote smuggling, but it will create cash flow problems for ZCCM which may restrict the ability to produce, and it will encourage smuggling of non-traditional exports and the re-export of imports obtained through official channels. On the demand side, there is no doubt that revaluing the Kwacha has led to an enormous increase in the number and amount of requests for foreign exchange. Comprehensive data on FEMAC'S activities are hard to come by but, for example, in weeks 18 to 22 the total amount of foreign exchange requested was $344 million while the amount granted under 'main applications' (i.e. other than own funds, export retention and PTA) was $51.4 million or 30 percent. In the five most recent weeks for which data was available (five non-consecutive weeks between 34 and 40) the total requested had grown to $409 million and the amount granted was $57.3 million or only 14 percent of total requests. In part this is no doubt indicative of the huge rents which can now be earned by those fortunate enough to gain access to scarce foreign exchange resources.

By the end of 1988, it appeared that the scarcity of foreign exchange was becoming more serious as firms complained that allocations approved in mid-November had still not been paid out (Times of Zambia, 2/12/88). At the same time, some Zambian leaders began to berate general managers of plants which closed down for lack of spare parts or raw materials, arguing that this was evidence of incompetent procurement!(Ibid, 30/11/88). A fourth disturbing indicator of growing economic woes is the inability of the government to reduce the fiscal deficit or to raise expenditures on vital social services in real terms. The weak revenue base of the budget is undoubtedly one of the biggest weaknesses in the government's attempt to implement an alternative adjustment program. The size and growth of the deficit are putting enormous pressure on the exchange rate and are making a mockery of the government's stated goal of reducing inflation rates. Revenue buoyancy was increased significantly by new tax measures introduced in 1986, including a switch from specific to 'ad valorem' duties and a widening of the commodity base of indirect taxes. Since then the government has raised user charges on a number of its services, e.g. in the health field, again raising important issues of equity. But, in spite of these revenue measures, the fiscal situation deteriorated notably in 1988. Neither the 1988 nor the 1989 budgets contain any significant additional revenue raising measures and it is unlikely that the buoyancy of the tax system or the growth in the economy will generate the 39 percent increase in recurrent revenue anticipated in the 1989 budget, high rates of inflation notwithstanding.

On the expenditure side, the IMF tends to argue for a reduction in general spending and in expenditures on subsidies. The irony of Zambia's good performance in terms of food production in 1988 was, of course, that expenditures on subsidies rose, by 70 percent! Abolishing subsidies at one stroke would almost triple retail prices (IMF,1988, p.18), and after the events of December 1986 is not a feasible proposition in political terms. The decision of the government to introduce a coupon system which would guarantee a minimum access to maize meal for all, while charging market prices for amounts in excess of the minimum, would effectively reduce the total subsidy and possibly reduce smuggling. This system was introduced earlier this year. It appears that access to coupons is limited mainly to urban dwellers. This would reduce the tendency of some peasants to sell unprocessed maize at pan-territorial prices and to buy maize meal for own consumption at the subsidised price, reducing in the process expenditures on the two-way transportation of food. It would, of course, also reduce cash income of such farmers, and reduce living standards of non-farmers in rural areas who previously benefited from the subsidy on all maize meal purchases. In addition, there are reports of abuse of the coupon system, but given the realities of Zambia's political economy, this is to be expected.

The government is attempting to reduce other expenditures by reducing the number of ministries from 21 to 16, by introducing economic rents for civil service housing and by turning the government stores into a parastatal (Budget Address, 1988). None of these measures is, however, likely to generate significant savings in the immediate future. Any other cut-backs in government spending would have to be evaluated carefully for their impact on employment and on the provision of basic social services which have apparently, already deteriorated to a dangerously low level, with particularly negative implications for the health and general well-being of women and young children (GRZ/UNICEF, 1986, and Muntemba, 1987). As will be argued later, it appears that a closer look must be taken by the government at raising tax revenues in future if its program is to hold together. This will also entail reviewing its exchange rate policy.

For the time being, one would have to conclude that the 1989 budget estimate of the overall deficit being reduced to K1.9 billion or to 5 percent of GDP, and therefore of the annual inflation rate being reduced to 30 to 35 percent, is quite over optimistic.

A fifth area of concern is that although the NERP was less austere than a typical IMF/World Bank adjustment program, there will undoubtedly have been some social costs. The continued erosion of social service expenditures must have been exacerbated by the withdrawal of foreign aid, although it is too early to tell what precise impact this might have had on the living conditions of ordinary Zambians.

The sixth area of concern is that of capacity utilization and employment. The sound growth in the manufacturing sector has led to some improvement in capacity utilization, but claims of significant improvements made in the INDP Progress Report No. 2 have been found to be quite exaggerated (Burdette, 1988 (2), pp. 7 – 9). Given the continuing tightness of the foreign exchange constraint, little improvement is likely. This means that recent growth in manufacturing employment, reportedly up from 48,860 in 1986 to 50,440 in 1988, or a gain of 3.2 percent is not likely to persist. Total formal sector employment, meanwhile, which reportedly grew by 0.35 percent in 1987 fell back to its 1986 level by the end of 1988 as the public sector shed labour. Unemployment in urban centres is expected to grow in the immediate future and a number of government training and settlement schemes designed to deal with this problem are unlikely to make much of a dent.

The sixth and final main problem area for the Zambian economy has to be the growing arrears of debt and the absence of any possibility under current conditions of Zambia coming to some kind of amicable arrangement with creditors. The result is a poisoning of relationships with hitherto, reasonably cooperative (if always somewhat skeptical) bilateral and multilateral donors. While, as we will argue below, this has not, apparently, cost Zambia any net foreign exchange flows to this point in time, since it has saved on its debt servicing, the situation can only deteriorate with donors becoming increasingly alienated, perhaps to the point where net losses are experienced.

Areas of success or promise

A disturbing aspect of the current situation in Zambia is the almost total opposition by donors to Zambia's attempts to develop its own adjustment program. So poisoned are relationships with the Fund and the Bank, and so influential are these institutions in the donor community that it is difficult for Zambia's policies to receive a fair and objective assessment. Yet there are a number of areas in which solid progress has been made by the government and a number of others in which progress promises to be made, often in the face of tremendous difficulty. Zambia is rarely given any credit for these efforts and often donors seem not to appreciate just how difficult it is politically for the government to deal with many of the economic problems it faces. What follows is an attempt to redress the balance a little.

First of all, Zambia has had great success recently in raising food production. Marketed output of maize has been much higher in all years since 1984 than it was previously. This was the case even in 1986-7 which was a drought year. In both 1985-6 and 1987-8, marketed output was in the region of 1 million tons, or about double the average marketed output in the years 1979 to 1984. While good weather played a role here, there can be no question that the structure of incentives was crucial. Table 5 shows that the government has, since 1980, kept real producer prices (nominal prices weighted by a rural price index, derived from the low income urban index by deducting food and related items and rent and related items) roughly at or significantly above their 1976 level. This stands in sharp contrast to policy in some neighbouring countries and is especially unusual when one considers that during much of this time Zambia was implementing an IMF program, which normally shifts terms of trade *against* food producers.

An important aspect of this success in food production is its impact on regional development, as it appears that income from maize sales now makes a significant addition to incomes in some less developed parts of Zambia such as the South, the East and the North and North-West. The introduction of maize has been a mixed blessing in the sense that it appears to have made increased demands on women's labour, and has also eroded dietary balance in some areas, but the money income gains seem to be unambiguous (Kydd, 1988). These gains would be threatened by the full-scale, sudden introduction of reforms being advocated by the Fund and the Bank, in particular the abolition of pan-territorial pricing and the closely related maize transportation subsidy, and the abolition of the fertilizer subsidy. Efficiency gains from these measures could, therefore, have serious negative income distributional costs unless reforms are approached carefully. The government's approach of slowly phasing out the fertilizer subsidy by 1990 is sensible in that it will give farmers an opportunity to adjust farming systems, but even here, no one seems to know what the overall impact of this will be on food production. Rationalizing grain handling to minimize transportation and handling costs, another of the government's current initiatives, is a sensible, long overdue move, whatever the policy toward subsidization and pricing. Any further reforms in this area designed to reduce the budget deficit ought to be preceeded by a careful analysis of the likely impact on regional income distribution and on total food output as opposed to export crop production. Thus, the abolition of pan-territorial pricing is likely to shift much maize production away from remote, high transport cost areas to the areas around the line of rail. It is not clear what would happen to output of crops currently grown in the latter areas, such as wheat, tobacco, soya beans and cotton. Likewise, it is not clear which crops would replace maize in the poorer, remote areas, although the theory would suggest they would be less bulky, higher value crops than maize: cotton has been suggested by some (e.g. Kydd, 1988, p.20), but it is not evident that adequate support systems exist to ensure a smooth transition to other crops. The likelihood is, therefore, that a rapid change of policy would undermine the regional balance gains made by the government in recent years, and with unpredictable impact on total agricultural output.

The second area in which current Zambian policies could be said to have had a measure of success is that of net foreign exchange availability. However unsatisfactory it may be to creditors and donors, limiting debt servicing to 10 percent of exports has probably *not* reduced the net amount of foreign exchange available to the country. The word 'probably' is used advisedly because it is hard to know exactly what resource flows would have amounted to if other policies had been pursued, but on the basis of admittedly sketchy data, it is highly unlikely that Zambia lost $640 million in aid last year, i.e. as much as it declined to pay in debt servicing or the amount by which its arrears probably rose. Gross loans from the World Bank (actually drawn as opposed to committed) would not likely have exceeded $75-90 million, based on the 1987 level of commitments (IMF, 1988, p.37), while the most that could have been expected from the IMF would have been a further $120 million or so. Losses from other donors are unlikely to have been greater than $100 million. It is difficult to estimate the amount of debt servicing which would have been rescheduled in any event, but the World Bank (1986 p.83) puts this at between $250 and 300 million for both the Paris Club and the London Club combined. It appears, therefore, that by limiting its debt servicing to 10 percent of its net exports, Zambia may even have raised its net inflow of foreign exchange by between $30 to $115 million above what it would have received otherwise. Even allowing for a margin of error (donors tend to exaggerate losses, Zambia to understate them), it is highly unlikely that Zambia has suffered a reduced inflow from its debt servicing strategy, at least to this point in time. Herein lies the attraction of the policy for Zambia and the dilemma facing donors and creditors.

In recent months the Zambia government has demonstrated that it is capable of flexibility and has taken a number of policy initiatives to address some of the concerns of donors. It *has* altered its exchange rate by 25 percent; it has raised interest rates; it has reduced the extent of price controls; it has introduced the voucher system for maize meal; it is rationalizing the structure and functions of government; it has raised user fees on government services; in 1988 it introduced guidelines for foreign investors giving considerable tax and foreign exchange incentives to companies producing non-traditional exports or using local products (Economist Intelligence Unit, 1988). This is not to endorse these measures, but rather to point out that Zambia has in fact moved some way in the direction advocated, rightly or wrongly, by donors and creditors. The skepticism by which these measures have been received indicates donor frustration with a government intent on following its own political agenda, and donor confidence, arrogance perhaps, that they have the solutions to Zambia's problems. Yet, the political situation in this country is highly volatile, there is widespread opposition to IMF-type policies and a history of violent protest against rapid adjustment involving further attacks on the living standards of urban wage earners. In this situation, and given the very real structural constraints facing the economy, viz. the supply constraints on copper, the unbearable burden of debt, and the very high import content of manufacturing (Loxley, 1988), the government *must* proceed cautiously, and donors ought to be counselling this rather than pressing for a speedy return to policies for which there is little political support.

This then raises the issue of what kind of policy changes ought the government to be considering, given the very real deficiencies of current policies outlined earlier.

Possible ways forward

Even if the Zambian government decides to continue to 'go it alone' in terms of its debt servicing policies, there are changes that ought to be made to its domestic policy.

a) There is a need for a cautious adjustment of the exchange rate. The current level is quite inadequate for ZCCM to make a profit and a contribution to the tax base. It is also too low to stimulate the promotion of non-traditional exports, and to introduce adequate incentives for import substitution, a major goal of the INDP. While some success has been enjoyed in import substitution at current overvalued rates, notably in the use of local fruit to replace soft drink syrups, there is a limit to what can be accomplished by the outright banning of imports or the mere exhortation to use local products. Ultimately, local costs have to be met and the level of the exchange rate is crucial.

Given the aversion to a return to the auction system, the way forward may well be the introduction of a dual or even multiple exchange rate, with official transactions (for such items as debt servicing, medical and school supplies, etc.) being conducted at a lower rate than other transactions. A fairly flexible rate could be used for imported consumer goods and non-traditional exports, while the rate for copper should be set so that ZCCM can finance its operations and capital expenditures at a reasonable rate of profit. The rationale for this is that a more flexible rate in some sectors would send the right kind of allocative signals while in others it would help the state absorb rents currently being earned by traders and others. At the same time, the use of different rates in different sectors would minimize inflationary stimuli and make budgetary adjustments easier to handle.

It is to be noted that there is already a precedent for the principle of multiple rates. At this time there are at least three official exchange rates operating in Zambia. There is the declared official rate, the rate at which export retentions are sold to third parties (all approved by the Bank of Zambia), and the rate at which pipeline debts (estimated at $400 million in 1988, Burdette, 1988) are sold to third parties. Both of these latter types of transaction involve implicit rates of exchange in the region of K25 per $US in 1988 (ibid). Then, of course, there is the black market with rates varying between K40 and 50 at the end of 1988.

Few in Zambia would recommend that the official rate be raised to that of the black market, but a strong case can be made for moving the flexible component of the dual/multiple rate gradually into line with the two other rates.

b) A thorough review of the buoyancy of the tax base is required in order to help curb excessive expansion of the money supply and to expand expenditures on health, education and basic social services. The target of this review ought to be the improvement of revenue collection, and an assessment of the incidence of taxation to ensure that the beneficiaries of current economic policies pay their share of taxes. Historically, Zambia has been noted for having extreme inequalities of income (ILO/JASPA, 1981). It is not known how the economic crisis in the 1980's has affected income distribution, except that urban wage incomes have clearly declined significantly (Young, 1988). The tax review would attempt to assess shifts in income distribution and ensure some equity in the system, although one can expect opposition to such an initiative from the Zambian elite.

c) The move toward limiting subsidies should continue, the object being to target them as much as possible to the needy. Over time, coupons ought to be gradually withdrawn from relatively higher income groups and focused on lower income groups. Rationalization of maize marketing and processing should continue in order to minimize transportation and storage costs, but caution should be exercised in reducing net producer prices to farmers for maize until more analysis is undertaken of its likely impact on total production, exports and imports. Agricultural policy should also seek to encourage a balanced diet among farmers in order to reverse dietary deterioration associated with recent expansion of maize production, and to ease the labour burden on women as much as possible. These issues are complex but deserve attention from government, perhaps assisted by donors.

d) The critical constraint on output in Zambia continues to be foreign exchange availability. If there is to be an accommodation with creditors and donors, however, they will have to offer Zambia much more than they offered in the period immediately preceeding the rupture of relations. Thus, the Paris Club consistently refused Zambia's request for multi-year rescheduling, and in 1986 granted it a 10 year rescheduling instead of the 15 years it requested. Furthermore, the World Bank (1986, p.86) has shown that at the London Club 'Zambia has generally been given more unfavourable terms compared to those obtained by countries with more serious debt repayment problems but without a meaningful reform program' e.g. the Sudan.

Even in the Bank's own projections in 1986, after assuming more generous rescheduling terms than Zambia had managed to obtain to that point in time, and an external financing gap of between $172 and $583 million to be financed by some unspecified source on concessional terms, the resulting debt servicing ratio between 1988 and 1991 was still between 44 and 68 percent! What these figures underscore is that Zambia's debt situation is completely out of hand and cannot be managed effectively given current constraints on the rescheduling of multilateral debt. Resolution of this problem will require extraordinary initiatives by donors and debtors: anything less will not suffice and Zambia might as well continue to set its own repayment terms.

The IMF (1988, p.24) has made balance of payments projections for Zambia based on the assumption that current policies continue. These show that if imports grow at 6 percent per year between 1989 and 1992, a financing gap of $430 to $480 million per year would need to be met if all scheduled debt servicing were to be paid. Since this gap is almost identical to non-ZCCM debt servicing, these projections would seem to suggest that, as the price of copper falls, Zambia will soon find it impossible to spend even 6 percent of its total exports on debt servicing without actually reducing imports below their inadequate 1988 level.

Looked at in another way, however, one could read these projections to mean that if Zambia continued to service only its ZCCM debt, and did not pay a cent to anyone else, it could still raise its imports in nominal terms, at a rate slightly in excess of the likely rate of world inflation, to 1992. It would, of course be accumulating massive arrears without any prospect of regularizing its situation with creditors, but it could survive and maintain current output levels. This conclusion serves to underscore the need for the international community to come up with an imaginative debt restructuring/forgiveness plan if Zambia is to be persuaded to regularise relations with its creditors and donors.

Conclusions

While the growth performance of Zambia has been reasonably respectable under the INDP, per capita incomes continue to fall, the black market is assuming unheard of proportions and inflation is very high. The debt servicing strategy of the government has probably not led to a loss of net foreign exchange flows, but creditors have become increasingly alienated as arrears mount without any plans to deal with them, and some donors are withdrawing support. Budgetary policy leaves much to be desired as rising deficits generate large increases in money supply, and as essential services are eroded. Food supply policies have, however, been very successful, with significant benefits to poorer regions, although at some cost in terms of allocative efficiency.

In recent months the government of Zambia has shown policy flexibility in a number of areas, even though the economic problems it faces do not lend themselves to easy solutions in political terms. Further changes are needed if negative developments in the economy are to be arrested and reversed. This will entail greater exchange rate flexibility, perhaps using dual or multiple rates, the creation of a more buoyant, hopefully more progressive tax system, and a cautious movement to reduce subsidies by targeting them to the poorer sections of society. These measures need to be undertaken for their own sake, but if donors and creditors wish to regularize relations with Zambia, they will need to recognize that in the past the flow of resources has been deficient. Extraordinary debt relief and aid flows are needed if the situation is to be rectified. If such relief is not forthcoming, then it appears from IMF projections that Zambia can tough it out alone, at least to 1992, with modest increases in imports, provided it pays only its ZCCM debt servicing commitments. The immediate negative leverage of the international community over

Zambia is, therefore, slight but there is enormous potential for positive influence provided an imaginative and enhanced financing package can be put together.

Part III

Moving in the IMF's shadow

9

Sparring
over
terms

By mid-1989 it was apparent that the government had begun to realize some of the above weaknesses of its 'go-it-alone' policies, especially the excessively rigid exchange rate policy, the overambitious attempt to control prices, the failure to control the fiscal deficit and money supply growth and the lack of prospects for breaking through the foreign exchange constraint in any significant way in the near future. On June 30th, President Kaunda announced an economic package which devalued the kwacha from K10 to K16 to the dollar (60 percent in kwacha terms, 37.5 percent in dollar terms) and removed all price controls except those on mealie meal. Wages, salaries and pensions were increased by 50 percent for low income earners and by 30 percent for the rest with effect from July. The coupon system for mealie meal was restricted to six dependents per family and to citizens earning less than K20,500 per year or K1,783 per month (US$1,300 per year). One week later, the price of mealie meal was also raised by 25 percent; breakfast meal to K70 per bag (25 kilo) and roller meal from K41 to K52.

On August 3rd the government implemented a currency reform replacing old notes with new ones. A tax of 50 percent was levied on amounts of old notes in excess of K10,000 handed in by other than the state sector, and a number of arrests were made at the border of people attempting to repatriate large quantities of old notes before the conversion deadline.

The objectives of this package of reforms were to rationalize the structure of relative prices, provide incentives to non-traditional exporters and to reduce the size of blackmarkets, tax evasion, etc. While, as argued above, something along the lines of these reforms would be essential if Zambia's 'go-it-alone' policies were to have any chance of success, many observers interpret them as an expression of desire by the government to regularize relations with the IMF, the World Bank and traditional donors (see, e.g. *The Economist*, London, September 30, 1989). This interpretation is based on the increasing frequency of contact between Zambian government officials and officials of the international institutions, as well as on President Kaunda's own statement, as he was announcing the reform package, that he was 'happy to report to the nation that they (the IMF and World Bank) have found... the measures taken by the party and its government since May 1987 to be a good basis for cooperation (Reported by Reuters, 2 July 1989). It appears, therefore, that the Zambian government is in the midst of yet another 'volte face' in its relationship with the IMF/World Bank.

For Zambia to regularize its status with the international institutions, however, it will need to find a huge sum of foreign exchange to pay off the arrears on IMF/World Bank debt servicing, estimated to have been in excess of $US 1.3 billion as of September 1989 (The Economist, London, Sept. 30, 1989). While in the past, the Scandinavian countries expressed some interest in assisting the clearing of arrears, the sums involved are now completely out of their range. Refinancing by the institutions themselves would appear to be the only feasible way forward. Yet this is unlikely to happen on the basis of Zambia's reform efforts to date. The IMF/World Bank would most likely insist on greater fiscal and monetary discipline. Money supply grew by over 70 percent per year between June 1988 and June 1989 and were this trend to continue, the whole point of the currency conversion exercise would soon be undermined. The IMF is also likely to demand more price flexibility and even further devaluation of the kwacha to keep pace with domestic inflation. Thus, while the devaluation was more than sufficient to reduce the real effective rate of exchange to below that of 1985 (by 11 percent – see IMF International Financial Statistics, January 1990, pp. 578-579), inflation is in all likelihood running, at more than the 1988 rate of 56 percent, and unless this can be brought down, the real exchange rate will appreciate rapidly. This underscores the need for fiscal and monetary reform.

It is imperative that improvements in the fiscal position be achieved without further erosion in the provision of health, education and social services and without more hardship on the urban poor. Since the early 1980s there has been a dramatic rise in the incidence of and death from malnutrition, malaria, respiratory infections and gastroenteritis. This is symptomatic of falling living standards and increasing poverty but also of the erosion of real government spending. Per capita real government recurrent expenditure on health fell by 42 percent between 1980 and 1987, from K12 to K7. In education, the fall in per capita spending between 1980 and 1987 was 60 percent (Andersson and Kayizzi-Mugerwa, 1989). UNICEF reports a rapid upturn in deaths related to delivery in the period of 1984 to 1987 which coincides with the heightening of the Fund reform programme. Equally, informed observers see no improvement and possibly even further declines in the 'go-it-alone' era, with the rigorous focus on production, continued pattern of corruption and siphoning of funds, and less concern with the issues of reproduction or social services in general.

The IMF will undoubtedly focus on reducing subsidy expenditure in the budget. Ideally, efforts should be concentrated on improving the efficiency of marketing and transportation by rationalizing NAMBOARD and the location of milling facilities. With adequate financial incentives and physical supports (credit, advice, etc.) some rationalization of production patterns regionally might also be possible which would reduce maize transportation costs. This must be approached carefully so that poorer farmers in more remote areas are allowed security of cash income. At the consumer end, the coupon system is still available to reasonably well-off families and over time this could be targeted to poor and middle income earners only. It is to be noted that the 25 percent increase in the price of mealie meal was not designed to reduce the subsidy but merely to offset, to some degree, the impact of devaluation.

The key to improving the fiscal position will, instead, lie in restructuring debt obligations and raising tax revenues. Unless the international institutions and foreign creditors are particularly creative in securing debt forgiveness or debt write-downs on a significant scale, it is unlikely that debt servicing payments will actually fall in the near future. The implication is, therefore, that revenue must be raised. In a context of falling per capita incomes this will be no easy task but as far as possible the extra revenue should be sought from the richer 50 percent of the population who appear to have roughly maintained their income share since the mid-1970s. Efforts should be made to tax those profiting from the crisis and those who have been able to offset salary falls by securing a large increase in various allowances (Anderson and Kayizzi-Mugerwa, 1989).

A reduced fiscal deficit will help reduce money supply growth but it is clear that credit to the parastatal and private sectors will also need to be restricted. This will be necessary if inflationary expectations are to be broken and overall efficiency of economic operations improved. The recent move to appoint an expatriate governor of the Central Bank, while deplorable as an admission of government failure and while smacking of a crude form of neo-colonialism, may in fact go some way toward restoring monetary balance.

It is too early yet to say how effective these new measures are likely to be. The essential political and social structure remains unchanged and hence the internal conflicts over policy are likely to continue. At this stage it would appear that technocratic pragmatists in the government have an upper hand, but so far the policy initiatives can be said to strengthen the ideas behind the Interim National Development Plan rather than replace it. A full scale IMF/World Bank program will require further austerity and further price liberalization. The pace and distributional impact of such measures will determine their political acceptability. The reaction of the union movement to 1989 reforms was not favourable as the wage and salary increases were insufficient to offset inflation rates prevailing *before* devaluation and price liberalization. They see these measures as a virtual return to the auction system, which will greatly reduce the living standards of ordinary workers, "creating a class society of haves and have-nots". (Sunday Times of Zambia, July 9, 1989).

Ultimately, the only logic behind yet another approach to the IMF/World Bank is that it will lead to a much greater inflow of foreign capital and, more especially, of real imports, than is possible under the INDP. So far, Japan has reacted favourably to last year's initiatives by providing $US24 million for the importation of vital raw materials, equipment and spare parts, making it clear that this was because of Zambia's new economic measures (Reuters, 15 December 1989). West Germany has formally converted US$310 million of debts into grants (Reuters, 26 November 1989). This move had been planned in 1988 but was postponed until the Zambian government implemented what the West Germans considered to be appropriate policy reforms. It remains to be seen whether other donors will follow Japan's lead and whether international institutions and other creditors have the flexibility to recast Zambia's debt obligations in a way that is at least as creative, in terms of limiting net outflows, as Zambia's own solutions under the INDP.

J.L.
Winnipeg, January 1990

Bibliography

Andersson, Per-Ake and Steve Kayizzi-Mugerwa. "Mineral Dependence, Goal Attainment and Equity: Zambia's Experience with Structural Adjustment in the 1980s" Department of Economics, School of Economics and Legal Science, University of Goteborg, Sweden, April, 1989.

Burdette, Marcia, M. "An Analysis of the Progress Report No. 1 of the Interim National Development Plan, Republic of Zambia" Prepared for CIDA, Ottawa, December, 1988.

"An Assessemnt of Progress Report No. 2 of the Interim National Development Plan, Government of the Republic of Zambia" Prepared for CIDA, Ottawa, December, 1988.

Chambers, Robert. "The Crisis of Africa's Rural Poor: Perceptions and Priorities". *IDS Discussion Paper, 201.* University of Sussex, February 1985.

Chilese, Jonathan H. *Third World Countries and Development Options: ZAMBIA.* New Delhi: Vikas Publishing House PVT LTD., 1987.

Development Committee. "Protecting the Poor during Periods of Adjustment". Number Thirteen, World Bank, Washington, D.C.

Economics Association of Zambia. "The Zambian Auction – A Documentation". Lusaka: July 1987.

Economist Intelligence Unit. " Zambia: Country Profile 1986-87". London: October 1986.

"Zambia: Country Report 1-1987". London.

"Zambia: Country Report 2-1987". London.

"Zambia: Country Report 3-1988". London.

Fundanga, Caleb. "Impact of IMF/World Bank Policies on Africa". Paper 25, Institute for African Alternatives, London: September 1987.

Good, Kenneth. "Systematic Agricultural Mismanagement: The 1985 Bumper Harvest in Zambia". *The Journal of Modern African Studies.* Vol. 24, No. 2, (1986), pp. 257-84.

Government of Zambia, *New Economic Recovery Programme: Interim National Development Plan,* Lusaka, July, 1987.

Monthly Digest of Statistics, Lusaka, Central Statistical Office, January-April, 1988.

National Accounts Statistics Bulletin, Lusaka, Central Statistical Office, January, 1988.

Economic Report, 1988, Lusaka, National Commission for Development Planning, December, 1988.

New Economic Recovery Programme – Interim National Development Plan, Program Report No. 2, Lusaka, June, 1988.

Budget Address, Lusaka, January, 1987.

Budget Address, Lusaka, November, 1988.

New Economic Recovery Programme: Interim National Development Plan, July, 1987 - December, 1988, Lusaka, July, 1987a.

New Economic Recovery Programme, Forth National Development Plan 1989-1993 Vols. I and II, Lusaka, National Commission for Development Planning, January, 1989.

Government of Zambia/UNICEF. *Situation Analysis of Women and Children in Zambia.* GRZ/UNICEF. Lusaka: June 1986.

New Economic Recovery Programme: Interim National Development Plan, Lusaka, July, 1986.

Helleiner, G. K. editor. *Africa and the International Monetary Fund.* IMF. Washington, D.C.: 1987.

International Labour Organisation (ILO)/JASPA (1981) *Basic Needs in an Economy Under Pressure: Findings and Recommendations of an ILO/JASPA Basic Needs Mission to Zambia,* Addis Ababa.

International Monetary Fund. "Zambia: Recent Economic Developments". Washington: October 1985.

"Report on Zambia's External Debt Renegotiation". Washington: June 1986a.

"Zambia-Overdue Financial Obligations to the Fund". Washington: November 1986b.

"Zambia-Overdue Financial Obligations to the Fund". Washington: January 1987a.

"Zambia-Overdue Financial Obligations to the Fund". Washington: March 1987b.

"Zambia-Overdue Financial Obligations to the Fund". Washington: May 1987.

"Zambia-Staff Report for the 1988 Article IV Consultation". Washington, D.C. June.

Institute for African Studies, "Analysis of the 1988 Budget of Zambia", Lusaka, University of Zambia, February, 1988.

Jalakis, Rudolf. "Foreign Exchange Zambia". SIDA Evaluation Report 1987/2, SIDA. Stockholm: 1987.

Kydd, Jonathan. "Changes in Zambian Agricultural Policy since 1983: Problems of Liberalization and Agrarianization". *Development Policy Review*. Vol.4, No.3, (September 1986).

"Zambia in Crisis" Critical Issues in the Agricultural Sector" Report to Swedish International Development Agency, September, 1988.

Lancaster, Carol and John Williamson eds. *African Debt and Financing*. Institute for International Economics Washington D.C.: 1986.

Loxley, John. *The IMF and the Poorest Countries*. Ottawa: The North-South Institute, 1984.

Debt and Disorder: External Financing for Development. Boulder, Colorado: Westview Press, 1986.

"Structural Adjustment in Africa: Issues of Theory and Policy" 1988 (mimeo).

Mijere, Nsolo N. J. "African Socialist Ideologies and the IMF Policies for Economic Development: The Case of Zambia". Paper to the African Studies Association. Los Angeles, California: 1986.

Muntemba, Dorothy Chiyoosa. "The Impact of IMF/World Bank on the People of Africa with special reference to Zambia and especially Women and Children". Conference on the Impact of IMF and World Bank Policies on the People of Africa. City University, London: September 1987.

Ncube, P.D., Sakala,M., Ndulo M. "The International Monetary Fund and the Zambian Economy-A Case". Uppsala: Scandanavian Institute of African Studies, January 1987.

Ndulo, M. and M. Sakala. "Stabilization Policies in Zambia 1976-85". ILO World Employment Programme Working Paper 13, Geneva: 1987.

Overseas Development Council. "Should the IMF Withdraw from Africa?". *ODC Policy Focus 1987*. No. 1, Washington, D.C.: 1987.

Price Waterhouse. "An Analysis of 1989 Budget Proposals", Lusaka, November, 1988.

Quirk Peter, B.V. Christensen, Kyung-Mo Huh, and T. Sasaki. "Floating Exchange Rates in Developing Countries". IMF Occasional Paper 53, IMF, Washington D.C.: 1987.

Smith, W. and Wood, A. "Patterns of Agricultural Development and Foreign Aid to Zambia". *Development and Change*, Vol. 15, No. 3 (1984).

UNICEF. *Adjustment with a Human Face*. Edited by G. Cornia, R. Jolly and F. Stewart. New York: Oxford University Press, 1987.

Van Donge, Kees. "Politicians, Bureaucrats, and Farmers: A Zambian Case Study". *Journal of Development Studies*, Vol. 19, No. 1, Jan. 1982. (October).

World Bank. "Zambia: Country Economic Memorandum: Economic Reform and Development Prospects". Washington, D.C.: November 1986a.

"Zambia: Policy Framework Paper". Washington: December 1986b.

"The World Copper Industry". Staff Commodity Working Papers. Number 15, Washington: 1987a.

"World Bank Programs for Adjustment and Growth". Discussion Paper, Development Policy Series by C. Michalopoulos, Washington: April 1987b.

"Issues Raised by Zambia's Debt Situation". Washington: July 1987c.

"Elements of a Special Action Program for Low-Income, Debt-Distressed African Countries". Washington: July 1987d.

Young, Roger, 1988, *Zambia: Adjusting to Poverty*, Ottawa, North-South Institute.

Tables

Table 1
Gross domestic product (at market prices in constant 1977 kwacha)

	1978	1979	1980	1981	1983	1985	1986	1987[a]
GDP (Million Kwacha)	1986	1937	1996	2119	2018	2080	2052	2095
REAL GDP (1978=100)		97	100	106	101	104	103	105
Real GDP per capita(K)	373	350	351	360	321	309	295	291
Real GDP per capita 1978=100		94	94	97	86	83	79	78
Annual % change		-6.2	0	2.6	-10.8	-3.7	-4.8	-1.3
Real GDP per capita ($)	560	490	446	414	256	114		

[a] Provisional
Sources: Government of Zambia, 1987a; World Bank, 1986a; and author's calculations.

Table 2
Gross domestic product (by type of activity)
(in percentages)

	1978	1979	1980	1981	1983	1985
Agriculture	16.1	14.9	14.2	15.9	14.2	14.5
Mining	12.7	17.6	16.4	14.0	15.3	14.2
Manufacturing	26.6	25.8	24.9	24.7	24.7	25.2
Services	43.1	41.2	41.8	42.8	44.9	44.2
Total	98.5	99.5	97.3	97.4	99.1	98.1

Note: Totals do not add to 100 percent. Residual is import duties.
Source: World Bank, 1986a.

Table 3
Balance of payments

	1978	1980	1981	1983	1985
Current A/C $ million	-141	-141	-863	-259	-191
Merchandise Exports $ million	1259	1259	1000	992	829
Merchandise Imports $ million	989	989	1238	839	752
Export Quantity 1980=100	100	–	79	78	66
Import Quantity 1980=100	100	–	125	85	76
Copper Output 000 ton	656	610	560	576	479

Source: World Bank, 1986a.

Table 4
GDP deflator

	1978	1979	1980	1981	1983	1985	1986
GDP Deflator 1977=100	113	137	153	165	207	304	486
Inflation Rate (%p.a.)	13	21	11	7	19	47	60

Sources: World Bank, 1986a and GRZ, 1987a.

Table 5
Index of the cost of living (1975=100)

	1978	1979	1980	1981	1983	1985
Low-income Urban	166	182	203	231	311	513
High-income Urban	162	173	196	229	328	528

Source: World Bank, 1986a.

Table 6
Domestic food production (000 metric tons)

	1978	1979	1980	1981	1983	1985
Cereals Maize	582	336	382	693	531	571
% Change Annual	–	-42	+14	+82	-23	+8
Oilseeds	11	15	22	24	28	50
Sugar	775	888	920	893	1010	1178

Source: World Bank 1986a and author's calculations.

Table 6.1
Index of maize producer price (1975=100)

	1978	1979	1980	1981	1983	1985
Nominal Value	136	180	234	270	366	564
Real Value (deflated by GDP deflator)	82	99	115	117	117	109

Source: World Bank, 1986a.

Table 7
External loans by type of creditor (commitment basis, US$ millions)

	1980	1984	1985
Bilateral	161.4	66.5	42.5
Concessional	133.4	53.8	42.5
Non-concessional	28.0	12.7	–
Multilateral	148.3	143.4	171.9
Concessional	84.0	25.2	152.5
Non-concessional	64.3	118.2	19.4
Private[a]	364.8	56.1	22.9
Total	674.5	266.0	237.3

[a]Includes official export guarantees.
Source: World Bank 1986a, p. 115.

Table 8
Real income trends (kwacha)

	1981	1986	1987
Watchman per hour	39	1.34	1.80
real wage	100	98.50	95.8
Labourer per hour	.44	1.39	1.85
real wage	100	90.6	87.3
Driver per hour	105	291	382
real wage	100	79.5	75.7
Clerk per hour	95	281	372
real wage	100	84.8	81.5
Tradesperson per hour	.49	1.44	1.71
real wage	100	84.3	72.9
ZCCM Grade 4 per hour	303	601	734
real wage	100	24	23

Source: *GRZ Gazette*, various.

Table 9
Central government budget (million current kwacha)

	1984	1985	1986
Total Revenue	1120	1602	3226
Income Tax	338	474	845
Customs and Excise	559	769	1437
Other	223	359	944
Total Expenditure	1485	2184	5384
Wages	451	536	661
Subsidies	90	188	570
Statutory Expenses	405	692	2252
Other Recurrent	354	488	906
Capital Expenses	182	278	993
Overall deficit	365	582	2158
Financing of Deficit			
Internal (non-bank)	36	68	59
External	67	109	529
Banking System	262	405	1570

Source: Ministry of Finance, Lusaka, 1987.

Table 10
Money supply growth (M2 basis)

	M2	% change	% change over previous 12 months
December 1984	1703		
March 1985	1681	-1.3	
June 1985	1731	3.0	
September 1985	1871	8.1	
December 1985	2104	12.5	23.5
March 1986	2504	19.0	49.0
June 1986	2713	8.3	56.6
September 1986	3185	17.4	70.2
December 1986	3456	8.5	
April 1987	5400[a]		116

[a]Provisional
Source: Government of Zambia, *Gazette Quarterly*, several issues.

Table 11
Interim national development plan: targets and performance 1988

	1987 Actual	1988 Target	1988 Actual
Real GDP Growth per year	2.2	2.2	2.7
– Agriculture	-2.2	1.7	6.4
– Mining	4.4	1.1	2.7
– Manufacturing	5.8	4.8	5.9
– Construction	-4.7	4.9	-4.7
– Services			
Real GDP growth per capita	-1.2	-1.4	-0.9
Real Gross Fixed Capital			
Formation (Km1977)	160.0	265.0	153.5
– As percent GDP	7.6	12.6	7.1
Real Final Consumption (Km 1977)	1880.3	1540.0	1843.8
– As percent GDP	89.3	73.5	85.3
Copper Exports 000 tons	475.5	470.0	419.1
Copper Price - U.K. pounds	1,078	900	1,372
Exports, Km	8015	6422	9554
Imports, Km	5639	5468	6043
Trade Balance, Km	2377	954	3511
Invisibles, Km	(3682)	(2273)	(4257)
Current Account, Km	(1305)	(1319)	(747)
Overall Balance, Km	(8609)	–	(10116)

Source: New Economic Recovery Program, Progress Reports

Table 12
Nominal and real effective exchange rates Zambia, *1979-1988*

	Real	Nominal
1979 Q1	103.6	95.7
1979 Q2	102.5	96.5
1979 Q3	101.1	97.4
1979 Q4	102.4	98.9
1980 Q1	101.2	99.7
1980 Q2	101.4	99.7
1980 Q3	99.0	100.0
1980 Q4	98.4	100.7
1981 Q1	97.8	102.1
1981 Q2	103.0	104.1
1981 Q3	104.0	105.4
1981 Q4	104.1	106.6
1982 Q1	106.2	109.5
1982 Q2	109.7	112.2
1982 Q3	116.6	118.5
1982 Q4	123.1	124.6
1983 Q1	104.8	104.6
1983 Q2	107.6	105.7
1983 Q3	107.6	103.5
1983 Q4	102.5	97.6
1984 Q1	92.5	87.5
1984 Q2	89.4	83.7
1984 Q3	90.4	82.1
1984 Q4	90.9	80.9
1985 Q1	91.2	78.0
1985 Q2	93.5	76.8
1985 Q3	104.4	81.1
1895 Q4	46.8	31.3
1986 Q1	43.0	26.5
1986 Q2	40.9	23.4
1986 Q3	48.9	26.2
1986 Q4	29.0	15.0
1987 Q1	31.9	15.8
1987 Q2	36.2	16.3
1987 Q3	50.0	20.8
1987 Q4	52.7	20.4
1988 Q1	58.3	20.8
1988 Q2	63.8	21.4
1988 Q3	76.1	23.6

Source: IMF

1980 = 100
A decline = depreciation
An increase = appreciation

Table 13
Zambia – central government fiscal positions 1987-89

'000K	1987 Plan	Budget	Actual	1988 Plan	Budget	Actual	1989 Budget
Total Domestic Revenue & Grants	4266	4792	4371	4143	5552	5687	7920
Total Expenditure	5735	6823	5537	5695	8302	8235	9838
Current expenditure of which:	4780	5615	4884	4862	6349	7535	7481
– subsidies	998	677	678	1115	2256	1152	1503
– interest	1048			702	1178		
– (External)	(152)			(128)	(217)		
– Capital Expenditure/Lending	955	1208	653	833	1953	700	2357
Overall Deficit	1469	2031	1166	1552	2750	2549	1918
– External net	398		(57)	1115	352		477
– Non-bank borrowing	50		41	63	70		67
– Bank borrowing	1021		1182	374	2328		1374
Percent Change in Money Supply			54			(Sep)51	40

Source: New Economic Recovery Programme, Fourth National Development Plan, 1988 Budget Statement

Table 14
Consumer prices - Zambia 1986-1988
percent increase per annum

Group	Low income group	High income group
1986 (Dec 85-Dec 86)	34.6	50.0
1987 (Dec 86-Dec 87)	50.5	50.3
1988 (Sept 87-Sept 88)	50.7	41.1

Source: Central Statistical Office, Lusaka

Table 15
Index of real producer price of maize 1976-1989 (1976=100)

Index	Nominal Producer Price index	Rural Consumer Price index	Real Producer Price index
1976	100	100	100
1977	100	121	83
1978	108	142	76
1979	143	156	91
1980	186	176	106
1981	214	201	107
1982	254	227	112
1983	290	273	106
1984	389	326	119
1985	449	450	99
1986	873	688	127
1987	1238	993	125
1988	1270	1533	83
1989	1714	1894	90

Source: Derived from Low Income CPI and Price Statistics supplied by Ministry of Agriculture.

Glossary

ADB	African Development Bank
CIDA	Canadian International Development Agency
DAC	Development Assistance Committee
EC	European Community
EDC	Export Development Corporation (Can)
EFF	Extended Fund Facility
ERP	Economic Reform Program
FEMAC	Foreign Exchange Management Committee
FNDP	Fourth National Development Plan
GDP	Gross Domestic Product
GNP	Gross National Product
GRZ	Government of the Republic of Zambia
IATA	International Air Transport Association
IBRD	International Bank for Reconstruction and Development
IDA	International Development Association
IFIs	International Financial Institutions
IMF	International Monetary Fund
INDP	Interim National Development Plan
NAMBOARD	National Agricultural Marketing Board
NERP	New Economic Recovery Program
PTA	Preferential Trade Agreement
SAP	Structural Adjustment Program
SDR	Special Drawing Rights
TAZAMA	Tanzania-Zambia Oil Pipeline
TAZARA	Tanzania-Zambia Railway
UNIP	United National Independence Party
ZCCM	Zambia Consolidated Copper Mines Ltd.
ZK	Zambian Kwacha